BLACK TRICKNOLOGY 101

CHARLES E. HILL III, M.S.

BLACK TRICKNOLOGY 101

Published by: Next Level Reading, LLC
Copyright © 2014 Charles E. Hill III, M.S.
All rights reserved.

Printed in the United States
Library of Congress

ISBN-13: 978-0692335413

ISBN-10: 0692335412

www.blacktricknology101.com

Cover Design: leoartist@gmail.com

Facebook: Author Hill

Blacktricknology101@gmail.com

CONTENTS

Dedications

This book is dedicated to a number of people who have had an influence on me, my life, as well as shaped my way of thinking. Family comes first as the foundation to have shaped me to be the man that I am today. In general I thank my family for being there for me in support outside of this project but for the everyday support as I grow and become wise on a daily basis. There are too many to name and those that have supported me know who they are.

Thanks goes out to the people who had an influence on my life from my youth growing up in Philadelphia, as well as my time at Scotland School for Veterans' Children. My time in Philadelphia as a child assisted in development in many stages. My experiences returning home in 2000 also shaped my experiences to grow mentally and develop the wisdom to understand in a different way of thinking.

To my Scotland family, I appreciate the support in life and also through this journey in trying to complete this project. As many have coined the phrase, "We are Scotland baby." With love to all those who have experienced the Scotland experience as I have. To this day I still receive the support from staff/administration, as well as the brothers and sisters from Scotland.

To the people whom I have met on this journey, the ones who have assisted me in this project through editing, illustration, and providing me with additional information that supported me in moving forward.

To those who have entered into my life for various seasons of growth and development. Life is about constant changes, experiences, relationships, various trials, and tribulations. Just because communication, contact, and experiences cease to exist, does not mean that lessons where not taken from them all. So I thank those whom added to my experiences of growth, knowledge, and wisdom.

Those who constantly communicated, debated, or asked questions in regard to my topics, work, and ideas, I thank you. Topics of discussion closed minded or opened assisted to fuel my fire to write as I have so again I thank you.

There are a lot of people and individuals who along the way continued to inquire about the completion of this project and encouraged me to continue to press forward, I thank you.

I also want to dedicate this book to those who struggle no matter the race, color, or creed. The on-going struggle continues bias of color but to status and ignorance.

Dedication has to go out to those who put their lives on the line to help, communicate messages of wisdom, knowledge, and freedom from bondage of what is not and has not been right for particularly Blacks in past, present, or for future generations. Though I say Black, there are many who are not Black that live life where equality is an issue as well. This is dedicated to those who seek knowledge and want to make changes in the name of equality.

I dedicate this book to families of those in the struggle whether, death, murder, prison, poverty, and all other problems associated with living within a system never designed for people not considered as equal. Continued knowledge, wisdom, research, education, and growth are the path for rightful understanding. I dedicate sincere thanks to all whom have even made it this far to read with open understanding.

In order to climb a mountain you need your ropes, supports, education, and anything needed to climb a tall mountain. As you climb to the top of the mountain there is another mountain and another. I equate the mountains to life. Each time you achieve or make it to the top, there is another obstacle or another mountain for which to climb. So imagine having to climb the mountains without the rope, without the help, support, education, and everything needed to climb the mountain, thus freedom from slavery. As the average individual not knowing how to climb a mountain one will either remain shackled in their limited conditions. Others will fail in trying non-traditional routes, while others will make their attempts in trying by way of survival. All too often the messages passed down from generation to generation is for families to survive, and why is that? One can only teach what has been taught, or what one only knows. And if people really focus to understand, Blacks as a whole has never had a full understanding of the American System. That is like playing a game for the first time not knowing the rules and your opponent understands the game in its entirety. Or running a race starting at the starting line and others has a massive head start.

In the 1950's and 60's there were movements and songs that suggest that we shall overcome. Martin Luther King once gave a speech illustrating his dream and his vision. As I observe present day Black America, there is no hidden secret that we have not achieved the mission to overcome as the past projected where we would be to this day. And why is that? With many questions and few answers, I decided to look deep inside of the reasons of why. Why are we as Blacks at the top of the list when it comes to the negative statistics within the American system? Why do Blacks continue to reside, as well as increase in numbers in the prison system? Why are conditions around the United States of America the same in just about all urban cities from state to state? Why are there too many homes where fathers are not present where women are left to raise the children, and/or the children are left to raise themselves? Why does there continue to be a rate of young parents by way of baby mothers and fathers? Why, why, why? There are many things that can be done to change the activities of behavior and actions, however things have not changed up until this point. One can see what I see and know that things are not getting better. And again I ask why? When people ask me about the content of my writing I share that I am writing about the things that go on with us as Blacks, the things that we do to us, and the things being done to us. I am in agreement that there are many things that are in our control and in our power in which we can change. I am also in agreement that there are many things that have been and still are against Blacks to this day. Our problems in Black America have been ignored and swept under the rag. Now with so many negative factors within the Black communities, the problems, conditions, and concerns can no longer be ignored. As people disregard past history and psychological barriers for Blacks, I embrace them. How much of the past has affected the minds of people to this day? If there is an open wound treated with a band-aid, will the wound heal? Though the wound will heal in some way but does that mean that the wound has been treated? Will that wound later become problematic? Thus present day Black America. From observation, communicating, and debating, I find that most Blacks have become comfortable being in, living and surviving in an uncomfortable state. Case in point, waking up each morning to attend a J-O-B (Just Over Broke), where one is disgruntled under the financial control of others. And why is that?

Introduction

"Just because you can perform a magic trick does not mean you are a great magician. It just means you have the ability to fool or create illusion in the mind of those who are either too dumb, too slow, or lack focus to see what is really going on."

-Charles E. Hill III, M.S.

The purpose of this book is to raise awareness around what occurs with us as Blacks, things that we do to ourselves and things that are done to us, which inadvertently affects us. In these pages, I want to address and touch on topics that most people do not focus on or discuss. The topics I address may spark dialog from time to time, however that's not enough. These topics need to be fully grasped in as much totality for us to have as much understanding of what is happening to us as Black

people.

To note, when I speak of Black people, I am also speaking about other cultures that live poverty stricken or have experience unfair injustice. Addressing Black issues is my passion, but also assisting people in changing mentally is a passion as well. We have been and continue to be tricked in many ways. We have been and are being conditioned to not think for ourselves. I want for us to gain knowledge, wisdom, and intelligence outside of the mental conditioning that is not helping us to become more than where we are. We need to know our culture, our history, and know who we really are. So many of us lack knowledge of self and live life in accordance to what is dictated by guided lines and "norms" set by society. I want adults to evaluate the conditions of their lives, to evaluate the legacy by which they live and govern their children, so that we take more appropriate measures and more appropriate steps to guide Black children in the right direction. Throughout the years, too much of our time has been spent in a negative light. I want to raise awareness of the negative factors that affect our lives as Blacks. I want Blacks to become better, to not allow things to continue as they have, so that our future generations will live in a better environment. We must make an effort to effect social change.

The context of my subject matter is not meant to offend anyone or any race. This is not a prejudiced approach that would condemn any particular race or ethnic groups. However, I would like to share my opinions because I feel they offer a more realistic view of what has been going on in society and in America regarding the situation of Blacks. I would like for Black people to take a stance and come together for the common goal of doing better. Like the late great Tupac Shakur said, "If I keep talking about how dirty it is, one day somebody is going to clean it up."[1] There are areas where I empathize with the situation of Black people, but there are also areas where our problems are self-inflicted. With that infliction, I will not always be sympathetic.

I realize that we have all too often been given the short end of the stick, being told all too often to be great without having much to be great with. It is like the movie *Friday*[2] when Smokey's (played by Chris Tucker) mother gave him money to buy cigarettes. Smokey told her, "Wait, wait, wait, this isn't enough," and his mother replied, "Make it enough." Basically, we have been getting muscled like Smokey; we have been told that despite the lack of resources and guidance, everything is "fair." As things continue to not be "fair," this lack has sparked me with the passion to write literature for the soul. Efforts should be made so that we can have a piece of the American pie and sit at the table to eat it.

While writing and formulating thoughts about the effects of the law, particularly the effects of prison, I recall a personal situation that provided more fuel to the fire. It was an incident with the police, county police at that. As a law abiding, taxpaying, educated Black man, the process of dealing with the police made for some interesting observations. Needless to say, I had the experience of feeling what is it's like to be treated as a criminal. On this particular day, I was stopped on the road for reasons I will not disclose. The policeman who stopped me was highly enthusiastic about completing his job to the fullest. I ended up in handcuffs and was asked to place myself within the back of the police vehicle. As a six-foot man, I found it impossible to sit in the back seat of the police car because of the amount of space and leg room needed. With my hands cuffed behind my back, I could not even get into the car by myself, and requested that the officer allow the handcuffs to be switched from the back to the front so that I would be comfortable to get into the car. He declined my request therefore had to slide backwards on my butt to get into the car.

On the ride to the station, I thought about how humiliating this was. I was thinking that all of my life I had avoided any type of confrontation with the police and have always talked with others about avoiding trouble with the law, but now here I was, all the same overwhelmed in thought. Upon getting to the station, I was not just told, but boldly told and directed in a loud voice where to sit, when to stand up, and so on. Although I am a grown man, the officer spoke to me as if I was a child. One of my hands was released, but the other remained cuffed to a long black chain that looked like the shackles formerly used for slaves. I asked the officer whether this was necessary and he suggested that it was. I remember thinking, *Man did I commit a murder or something?* The officer explained that it was necessary to keep me cuffed for twenty minutes. When that time had passed, I was released from the one-arm handcuff.

After the handcuffs were removed, I was asked all kinds of questions, and answered them respectfully, if at times sternly, with "yes sir" or" no sir". I was told when to get up and where to sit down.   When I asked the policeman if I could use the restroom, I was told that I had to wait for him to finish his report and complete the other questions and procedures needed throughout this process. After he was done, I again asked if I could use the restroom. Because he claimed there was a mix up in the processing, I had to wait even longer. Only when he had finished completing all these tasks was I able to use the restroom.

Before I go any further, I want to say that I am not trying to justify my actions that night or to suggest that I was not in the wrong. When you are in the wrong, you have to own it and accept what comes your way. Without getting into the particulars, what occurred that night sparked a blaze of fire for me to write, which I did.

Throughout the processing, I asked if I would be able to speak freely and was told that I could. So, I told the officers that I intended to write a book and would include this particular incident. I am certain that they did not believe me. I told the cops that I was writing about the situations of Black people and what we go through. I began to list and discuss the topics I intended to write about: "Why is it that there are more Black men in prison than there are in college?" "Why is it that, although a criminal who becomes educated in prison is less likely to return, as there is no funding for education of prisoners, but there is always money to build new prisons?"

Of course they did not have any answers, and frankly I am certain that they did not give a s@#$. You can fill in the blank on that one. But, I also began to ask why all of our Black leaders are murdered and never die a natural death. Of course, they did not know that answer nor did they know most of the leaders I mentioned, such as Huey Newton, Malcolm X, and Bunchy Carter. Again, I am certain that they did not care at all. I told them that I had never before had a problem with the law, but with this experience I felt I got treated like a nigga.

Although I was not detained, I asked if I could stand in a jail cell. I did that only because I wanted to see what it was like. Just as Alex Haley rode the slave ship in order to feel what the slaves had experienced, I too wanted to get a small taste of what it was like to be in a prison cell. The conversation continued with the police for a little longer until I was released to leave. Of course, now that it was time for me to go, the cop became a little more cordial. I told him that I would remember this night and also that I would put his name in my book, as I spelled it out from his badge: S.A. Sanger from Lancaster County. I told him that I would send him a copy of the book once it was done. He thought I was joking; in fact, he gave me his card and suggested that I keep it. He expressed the hope that I would not forget, and I did not forget the way he and his young dispatcher Adam (who at first refused to give me his name, and even then never gave me his last name) brushed me off. As I was leaving for the night, Officer Sanger said that if there was anything that he could do for me to please let him know. *"You freakin' jerk"* I thought, *"if you had something you could have done for me, you would have done it by now."* Here's to you, S.A. Sanger of Lancaster County of Pennsylvania. Thanks for giving me a taste of penal code treatment of what most Blacks experience.

Chapter One

<u>LIFE</u>

Life is broken down as:

"Lessons/Incorporated/From/Experience."
                              -Charles E. Hill III, M.S.

Sometimes a race can be run without ever crossing the finish line. Sometimes a race has already started while you were at the starting blocks, unfairly disadvantaged and most likely unable to catch up to those who have already started. In the 1950's and 60's, there was a song that goes, "Deep in my heart, I still believe, that we shall overcome some day." Have we overcome since that song was sung? Or have we taken steps further back in time? There are still many factors within our community, within us as Blacks, African Americans, or whatever you want to call yourself, that from generation to generation have not overcome the obstacles placed before us to what we have sought to achieve. A question that I often ask myself is: Where have we gone, and where are we going? Observing "we" as a people, I see so many elements and factors within ourselves that keep us confined to our present situation, so that we never move from the current situation to where we want to go. From observation, I can see that "we" are in trouble. I see that "we" are definitely cursed, whether consciously or unconsciously.

When I speak of a curse, I am speaking of a generational curse,

which is defined as: "judgments that are passed on to individuals

because of sins perpetuated in a family in a number of

generations."[1]

There are many psychological factors that help to keep us

stuck in a continuous destiny of going nowhere. The end of slavery

(not implying that slavery is indeed over) does not mean the final

end of the pain and harsh experiences that we have endured. But

just because something is over, does that mean it is instantly erased

from the mind? *Think about it*, 400 plus years of conditions that

were inhumane, painful, and psychologically damaging infringed on

us against our will. Imagine a person who has been not only

physically abused, battered, beaten, but mentally abused

(brainwashed) as well. The psychological abuse is just as powerful,

if not more so than the physical. Psychological abuse means that

someone has gotten into your thoughts to make decisions, which

means the way that you think is out of your control in the same

manner that a person's mind may be controlled by a substance.

Under the influence, your mind is not yours; you are controlled to

do what you do not want to do. When you are broken down

psychologically, self-esteem, respect, pride, and your overall outlook on life is damaged.

Black folks have been both psychologically and physically abused. The true embodiment of who we are and what we want to be has been lost. Now clearly, there has been a change for a large number of Blacks in America. It is apparent that a vast number of us have achieved success by the fruits of their labor. This is evident by the number of successful Blacks who have made opportunities for themselves. Although I agree that there are many who have achieved success, those who have been able to do better for themselves is still a small percentage and I do not want to lose sight of the overall population that have not been able to do so well. Being thrown bones and scraps does not mean that we are eating. The majority of the Black race tends to not be afforded the same success or means to obtain even the scraps to eat. I believe that we would have made out better if we would have gotten what had been promised to us by way of reparations: 40 acres and a mule—a promise that has never been kept and a benefit that we will never receive. Instead, we have been given lies—bad lies at that. Although we worked hard and built this nation and its economy, we never received any benefits from it, despite being promised a fair share.

With regards to mental enslavement, there are many individuals who have not been able to make the jump from the post slave mentality (post-traumatic stress/trauma) to become highly successful within the American system. I am not saying that an individual should sit back and talk about how it was to be a slave or the fact that slavery is the reason why they cannot get a job in present day society. Though there are many problems in the Black community, these issues affect us from generation to generation, and of course this has something to do with the mental enslavement and sense of entrapment passed down from generation to generation.

For example, there are individuals who do not receive or provide love within a family setting. I asked a parent of a child that I worked with at a school, to tell her son that she loves him, and she replied that she could not do that. I was shocked to find a woman who could not express love or feelings to her own children, shocked and amazed by her comment and by the blank stare that indicated she was serious. Then I thought *how does this work for the benefit of the children?* As I think back and analyze parents and children that I have worked with over the years, I come to the sad conclusion that there are a lot of children who live in households where they are not loved, more than most people can imagine. I do not mean to imply that this is just a woman's problem; it is the responsibility of the father as well. Men will too often produce a child and then have nothing to do with the child. Now where is the love in that? It is also not uncommon in the Black community for families to be unable to express their feelings by saying "I love you." When and where did that start?

I gave the matter considerable thought. There must be various factors that contribute to such lack of love. Where did that come from?   No research will be able to determine exactly where it started or give an official date, however it is known that almost everything we learn or do operates within the particular environment in which we live. If there was no love or expression of love at home, most likely my household will not express love either, unless it has been learned, experienced, or developed elsewhere. Did the home where my parents grew up express love?

Now keep going back and back, to generations that grew up in slavery. For instance, why is it that Black households beat their children as a form of discipline more often than do other ethnic groups? *Think about it*: How did master discipline us as slaves? Master would beat us. So in turn, we adopted that as the form of discipline for our children. A similar case is that most of our young women have children at an early age. Where did it start? During the period of slavery, this was when the young slave women would have children at an early age. These women would have multiple children as well. Now in present day society, please tell me, does the same situation still exist? Why is that? It is a psychological attachment/curse and many in the present generation still have not been able to grasp or understand how to break out of that curse.

Prison and going to jail is another such curse. Defying and running from the law was indoctrinated into the slaves by our culture. Though slavery was the law—and a bad, inhumane law—all in all it was still the law. Stiff penalties were applied to those who broke this law, but it was also natural that Blacks would rebel against such laws. As bad as this law appears to us today, defying the law meant stiff penalties regardless of its injustice and inhumanity.

Because of this history, there are many families in the Black community that come from a long line of persons, mostly men but women as well, who have spent time in jail. Again, where does it come from? More importantly, will it stop? To live life in defiance of the law means to live in accordance with one's own personal code of ethics. That code is exemplified as what is right for individuals at that time, even though it defies the law. For example, slavery was a law, but slaves wanted freedom. So in order to step outside the law, slaves tried to obtain freedom. Some individuals see selling drugs as the only means to make money, so they defy the law. There are some people that have not made the appropriate choices in life to function within the system and, as a result, they would rather defy the law for a beneficial gain then to continue to starve. I realize that many people do not live their lives in accordance with the law of the state or the system and I do not suggest that either way of living is wrong. Though society and the system is greater in numbers that does not mean the system is right. For example, just because slavery was the law does not mean that it was just. Simply because a judge or jury suggests that a person is guilty (or not guilty) does not mean the decision was right. Is it truly "just" or justified by the system? And the system is not designed for the benefit of Blacks; it never was and still is not in the best interest for Blacks. So I ask, how can someone Black have a fair trial when they are judged by a jury of their peers, which includes no one who looks like, talks like, or has ever lived like the individual on trial?

One thing that we as Blacks need to understand is that no help or real assistance will benefit Black people unless we help ourselves. In other words, you cannot rely on the government to repair the neighborhoods. You cannot rely on the government to make the educational system better or even equal to the schools in more affluent areas. If we do not help ourselves, who will? This needs to be made clear and understood. If I am wrong in what it is that I am speaking, please show me the light. I do have to credit groups and organizations (including those run by persons from other cultures) that have and are willing to put their lives on the line for equality. Various accounts of history and documentaries have shown this, but the base is very small compared to the overall masses in society. However, the main burden of the work that needs to be done falls to us as Blacks. When I say that no help exists, I am speaking about the government's overall approach to Black assistance for the betterment of Black people. I am not saying there are not individuals who fight, but that fight is lost because the system is greater than the individuals that join in the fight, or better yet not enough fighters to where change is made. The system benefits from the failure of Blacks, Blacks being poor, reduced education, no Black leaders or direction, and lack of Black organization. The jail system/slave labor (i.e., work for prisoners), and the welfare system are all government programs that benefit if you fall within the negative categories of society. Yet programs that benefit Blacks are cut as the economy continues to decline. When

things get tight within education or human service
organizations, there are no bailouts like there were for Wall
Street. There are no bailouts or anything else for the benefit
for Blacks.

Another important topic for the Black community is the
question of leadership. Since Malcolm X, Dr. Martin Luther King
Jr, and the Black Panthers, who have "we" had as leaders to direct
us in leadership? By leaders, I mean those who can bring the
people together to create true power that will enable us to go
further. Over the last few years, I have a new-found respect for Al
Sharpton. He has some form of leadership to have helped others
at some time. So there is some leadership being provided, but
none that has helped to shift us from where we are, to where we
can, and where we should be.

Tupac Shakur once said, "None of our leaders ever die by
natural causes, but by murder." Similar to this is the anonymous
saying, "If you cut the head of the leaders, the rest will scatter."
Think for a minute about the consequences of the deaths of
Martin, Malcolm, and Huey Newton (founder of the Panther
Party). When these individuals were living, there was a plan, a
direction, and an agenda. The importance of such leaders is

brought home in the movie *Glory*. Denzel Washington plays a soldier who is next in line to carry the United States flag, if the original flag bearer gets killed or injured. In the story, when the original flag bearer dies, Denzel retrieves the flag and leads the troops forward for a fighting chance at victory, enabling them to continue to move forward with the agenda. Needless to say, Denzel was killed as well, but the moral of the story is that once the strong and powerful leaders were murdered (because all of them were), there was no one in place to pick up the flag or agenda and move us forward. As a result, we scattered, living our lives in a manner that led to where we are today.

    To take another example from film, in the documentary *Bastards of the Party*[2], the narrator "Bones" wanted to find out the origin of the Bloods and Crips gangs. The documentary shows that while the Black Panthers were in place, they were able to give us some organization as a people. While the Black Panthers were strong, we didn't see the violence and destruction in our communities that we see today. But once there was an infiltration of the party, the rest (we) scattered to what? After Huey's death and the destruction of the party, the documentary depicts how the Black community changed, descending from unification to a downward spiral of self-gratification. Drugs became common and those who wielded power in the community were no longer leaders, but pimps and drug dealers. No longer could we say as a people, "I'm black and I am proud." The documentary also suggests that as drugs began to flood the neighborhoods, the image of us as a people began to change as well. When the Panthers were up and running, Black music and the depiction of Blacks in movies were different. James Brown sang songs like "I'm Black and Proud" and movies depicted us as strong Black men and women.

Once there was no longer unity, it became easier to change the structure of the Black community and the way we did things. Movies and songs shifted from pride to self-glorification and their characters were now pimps and drug dealers. Their soundtracks reflected the mass production of drugs within neighborhoods around the United States. And by neighborhoods, I do not mean Beverly Hills. I mean neighborhoods where there is less money, less hope, and fewer resources, making it easier for drugs to be consumed by sellers or users.

Could that have been a calculated, orchestrated, well thought out plan to pull us back from the "promised land" where we were headed, the "promised land" of Dr. King's

American dream? Like a train trying to reach its destination, we have been derailed and knocked off course. If the train does not get back onto the track, it cannot reach its original destination. Our train has been knocked off track and has never returned, to adverse effects. As result of the continuous "tricknology" (as I call it), as well as a lack of oversight and understanding, we fall for anything.

For example, there is a huge drug problem within the United States, and we (Blacks) conspire to be a part of it. Our communities are flooded with drugs for which we rob, steal, and kill in order to acquire power and fame. This means that we fight and kill each other for this evil resource that destroys our communities, families, and lives. I do not hear about white on white crime, but I do hear about Black on Black. Why is that? Although things appear to have gotten better for some Black people, the Black communities as a whole have not achieved the same success and things are not better compared to other ethnic groups. And in observation, the gaps of better, positive change, has never reached a level of equality or even close to equality.

Now understand the use of "tricknology" that continues to plague us to this day. As we were freed from slavery, we were freed into what? Tricknology. *Think about it.* Slaves were not educated, did not have money, or a place to go. Nor, for the most part, was there accessibility to a job market that would hire former slaves to

live equally within society? So, although the legal victory over

slavery was fought and supposedly won, it was not a true

victory. If you research and check the history, when Blacks were

set free from slavery, it was only a glorification with

consequences in reality. And how long did that glorification last

before reality set in? Though slaves were deemed to have

freedom, freedom did not equal fair or fairness. Furthermore,

this freedom did not come with ownership of anything but

reliance on Whites and other Slave Masters. After the realization

that a free uneducated slave had no idea how to make it within

the current American system, many would resume work at the

same plantation or a similar plantation from which they were

"freed" from. Know that the law did not obligate responsibility;

the owner did not have to pay the worker for work.

    In the documentary *Booker's Place: A Mississippi Story*[3],

elder Black men and women discussed life after slavery had

ended. One gentleman discussed the work of sharecropping. He

suggested that work was not done from 8:00a.m.-5:00p.m,

normal working hours. He shared that work started when you

could not see and ended when you could not see, meaning that work was done all day. Then the man broke down the payment options, expressing that at the end of the year when it was time for the workers to be paid, if the workers completed about four more bundles of cotton, then they would have broken even. This leaves the impression that each year the sharecroppers were always in debt, a debt that would never get paid, so basically slavery continued. So I say again, though slaves were deemed to have freedom, freedom did not equal fairness or the end to debt paid slavery.

A vast number of incidents suggest that things never were fair and never will be. When I observe the mistreatment of President Obama compared to other presidents, I can see that treatment is not fair. When I see the lives of Emmett Till, the case in Mississippi (three civil rights members killed), the not guilty verdict of George Zimmerman and more Blacks murdered under *Stand Your Ground Law*, I can see that justice continues to have a blind eye where Blacks are concerned. In other words, unfair. For those that do not know the name Emmett Till, he was the boy who was killed in 1955 for whistling at a white woman. In the mid 1960's, three civil rights members were murdered in Mississippi, an incident that inspired the movie *Mississippi Burning*. Some may say these events happened so many years ago that we should just forget about it. But I bring these events to your attention to share the history of injustice toward Blacks in the United States, which continues to this day. The murders of Emmett and the civil rights workers in Mississippi ended with those accused and convicted receiving little to no jail time, even though the evidence and witnesses suggest that they did in fact commit the crimes. Similar cases are Rodney King and the murder of Trayvon Martin.

In the case of Rodney King, there was taped evidence and still no conviction. Trayvon Martin's case lacked conviction due to an unjust *Stand Your Ground* law that set a man free who should not be. And I might add that the law still has not been changed, which resulted in more Black murders. I use these isolated incidents to prove my point that justice is unfair for Blacks. The case of Mumia Abu Jamal is another situation where injustice continues. The story of the Jenna Six members in Louisiana records injustice as well. Though all of these stories are public knowledge, there are countless others that have not been reported. Another issue within the U.S. justice system is the many trials where the law is clearly violated when it comes to Blacks. For example, the law states that an individual will be tried by a jury of his/her peers. If that is the case, then why should a Black man or woman be tried by an all-white jury? But has there ever been a case where an all-Black jury tried an individual who is white? I would love to see research showing an instance of that and if it has happened, how few in comparison? All in all, we must conclude that this is, "not fair."

In discussing the issues and concerns I have with our situation as a people, I have encountered individuals who feel that my views are an invitation to stay stuck in the past. Some people say that talking about the past associated with slavery/past history and all other negatives that has affected us, in consequence can too easily be used as a crutch to excuse us for not moving forward. But I must respectfully disagree. I believe that our past and what has happened should never be forgotten, should be discussed, and analyzed to determine how things are synonymous to have not changed to this day or to understand what barriers still exist in present day society.

Just as American history recounts the experiences of the great settlers and the accomplishments of Anglo-Saxons, so too should it recount our stories, our accomplishments, and our tragedies. I believe that "you live but you never forget". Why is it wrong to talk about the past or to debate the parallels between where we have come from and where we are now? The stories of great Black innovators, revolutionaries, and countless others should never be swept under the rug. But in the schools we attend, our stories are never told.

Unless we are taught at home, Blacks are exposed to a limited amount of Black history, which should be rightfully classified as American history. History is not fair, at least where it concerns the distribution of resources allotted from one race to the next. If Blacks/African Americans are considered Americans, then shouldn't our history be considered American history? Why should it be separate? Our story is not only our story, but part of American history. African American/Black history and the contributions of Black Americans should be included in the school setting just as much as Anglo-Saxon American history and contributions. History teaches us to "know thy self," and that is a major reason for its importance, knowing one's self and heritage is valuable. If a person does not know where he or she comes from, how can they know where they are going? And to this day, do we as Blacks know our history; know ourselves, or even where we are going?

This loss of direction and lack of self-knowledge accounts for the many lost souls of today's generation who exhibit signs of arrested development, meaning that the individual has not developed to the appropriate level of maturity where he or she can function as a responsible adult. The Urban Dictionary further defines a woman child as "an immature infant trapped inside the body of a grown woman," which is in the context of woman-child[4]. I would presume that this same definition holds true for a man-child. The state of arrested development is "a state where development has stopped prematurely"[5]. If we are honest, we must admit that there are a lot of individuals in communities who exhibit signs of arrested development. I see men, and even women, with their pants sagging; I see parents who lack interest in taking appropriate care of their own children or giving them appropriate guidance. The sheer number of irresponsible sexual acts where neither individual gives thought nor concern for what happens after the fact is yet another sign of this lack of understanding. I can easily spot such persons: physically, they appear to be adults, but they lack maturity.

Now I will admit that even the most mature individual may lack development in certain areas of life. However, to remain in a state of arrested development is to remain shackled, locked up in thought to the point where the realities of life pass you by and you are mentally chained from moving forward. I do not think that we focus on why this problem is important, but we should. We should because there are generations after generations of developmentally arrested families that do not break away or try to educate their minds beyond the immature level of their arrested development.

All this goes back to the way that history is presented to us. We as Blacks need to understand and acknowledge that the way history is depicted in American society brain washes us and keeps us stuck. History is broken down as **_his-tory_**, the story is told from the limited perspective of those in the dominant culture within America. For example, in school I learned about the settlers and the Indians. A really good packaged story. But as I grew older, I learned that the stories we were taught in school is not the true story by any means. Now why is that? I know that the Indian community has shared their stories, so there is no excuse for present-day society to claim ignorance of what really happened or for present-day textbooks to omit the Indian interpretation of events, which tells the story from a different aspect.

So why is it that history textbook presenting the stories of American Indians, African Americans, and others whose voices were not previously heard have not been changed to relate what really occurred? It is because if you ever tell a lie, you have to tell another lie, and then additional lies to cover up the first one. Sometimes you tell a lie so much that you start to believe it yourself. These lies were told to cover up the brutality, unlawfulness, inhumanity, and other forms of oppression committed by the dominant race. In essence, the truth hurts, and perhaps those who write textbooks fear the truth will show that those who appeared to be great may not have been. The true history of the Indians shows that they were betrayed, sucked dry of their kindness, hospitality, resources, and knowledge.

Of course, that story will never be told within the school setting. Nonetheless, it is the truth. Those who were the least righteous are most often glorified as great in the eyes of American history and we continue to teach those lies and deceptions and pass them off as history. History repeats itself because current "history" as depicted in textbooks and popular culture presents current lies to the current generation: for example, the events behind 9/11, the fiction that the Iraq war resulted from that country's manufacture of weapons of mass destruction, and other events that are presented from the slanted perspective of "his-story" are all current interpretations of untrue events, just as history of the past. Yet the events are another form of tricknology and mind control. It will be interesting to see how the story of President Barrack Obama is presented in the history books of the future. From what viewpoint or perspective will it be depicted, as true history or as falsified "his-story"?

Chapter Two
Survival

As a wise man once said, "The history of the world, my sweet, is who gets eaten and who gets to eat." That's *survival* in a nutshell. It's the act of continuing to live, usually when others fail.[1]

What is the difference between living and surviving? What is it to have and have not? If we wish to understand the Black struggle and why we continue to struggle, these are questions that should be examined. The basic definition of "survival" is a continuation of life despite difficult conditions; a "survivor" is one that survives.[2]

There are individuals who live by the adage "If you fail to plan, then you are planning to fail." Making a plan means creating a blueprint of what needs to be done, a blueprint that includes making a plan and setting goals which illustrates a path that will give direction and hope to end up at an intended destination. This blueprint can then be studied, analyzed, tweaked, and changed if additional steps need to be implemented in order to achieve one's goals. The end result may not always match our initial goals, but the process of creating and implementing a plan may give us new ideas and influences. The new ideas can introduce us to helpful people and factors, and spark a new direction that can lead to other areas of success.

Survival, on the other hand, is not a plan but a form of nature. Human nature, for instance, requires the basics of food and water as well as clothing and shelter. But what happens when individuals do not get their basic needs met? Some become lost within society: the homeless individuals who ask for money, whom most of us simply avoid in our everyday travel, do lack in obtaining basic needs in the scoop of society.

People become homeless through either forced or unforced circumstances. But other individuals decide that homelessness is not an option for them, and acting under this mindset, such individuals will find alternative means to survive. The tactics used by such persons generally result in crime or other immoral activity, all in the service of obtaining material benefits that will enable them to survive. These material benefits usually center on money or other intangibles that involve money. In many cases, this struggle to survive is at the root of drug dealing and other crimes.

Although I oppose drug dealing, viewing it as harmful and a detriment to the Black race, I understand the path and the mindset that leads to embracing it as one's lifestyle. For a child particularly a male, with ambition but no money and no opportunity or belief of making it within the American system, what other options are available? For such a child, school does not appear as much of an opportunity to provide himself with the financial means that will assist in achieving a better lifestyle.

Put yourself in the shoes of many Blacks who have lived under adverse conditions with no alternative means of getting out. How can you judge or suggest that living within the system is not considered a trap? Living within the system means living at the bottom for many Blacks/African Americans, hence observation of Black communities from generation to generation, state to state. At home, bills are due; lights and electricity are on the verge of being cut off. There is a lack of food and other resources, creating tension at home. In most homes, mothers are the single provider and work hard to provide, but in the end, the ends do not meet. There is very little help or support for mom, so she is always mad and angry. Because mom is out at work, maybe working two jobs just to put food on the table, there is a lack of parental input as needed for the child/children. Since mom is not home, the older siblings are left to raise the younger children or the children are raising themselves. This is where education can become lost, if education is not already lost at this point.

When a kid/child/adolescent sees his mother struggling over the course of the years, a young male, and at times female, realizes how detrimental this is to their family. To assist in some of the responsibilities at home, in most cases the male within the household will look to obtain financial gain for himself and his household. However, there is very little, moral means of obtaining sufficient money to assist in survival at home. Due to the young man being young, uneducated, and not having an opportunity to work for decent wages that reflect his efforts, the individual looks to other possibilities. Of course, the notion that crime and drug dealing is a viable way out of his current struggles and situation is an illusion. Yes, money can be made from drugs and other criminal activities, but at what price in the end? How much is your life worth?

A good friend of mine, who has spent some time in jail, shared that he would not wish jail on his worst enemy. Other words of wisdom shared by a former drug dealer who also spent time in jail when he was younger shared that he has to remind himself at work on a daily basis that "slow money is still good money." So while crime and drug dealing may be forms of survival, it does not breed anything positive in the end. If I may speak to young people who are simply trying to survive, I would advise you to switch gears, to avoid the pitfalls and traps that set you up for failure. Though the struggle is hard, try to rise above your current situation by planning for a more positive outcome that does not land you dead or in jail, or enslaved to crime and other trappings of the game.

Survival is also the natural heritage that has been passed down from one generation to the next and that same survival mentality continues to cripple us to this day. Survival has become so deeply rooted within our culture that by now it seems to be all too natural; we do not know anything else. But where did this survival mentality start? When I speak of survival, I am not suggesting in any way that we not strive to obtain something for ourselves. However, I would like for as many of us to move past the notion of just surviving to making it in life. If we look back to the historical moment when we were "freed" from slavery, we can see where and how survival began. The act of freeing slaves from the plantation has been viewed as the redemption of slavery's curse, transforming it into a blessing. A blessing because Blacks were no longer slaves, obligated to work on the plantation for nothing, where we would no longer be beaten, raped, starved, and killed.

However, once we were free, what was the basis of freedom? If you think about it, the slaves were set free only to walk away from the only lifestyle they had ever known. What knowledge or understanding did they have about the current American society at that time? What opportunities existed for Blacks? There were no programs such as shelters or housing developments that provided help and assistance to former slaves seeking refuge until they could get on their feet. There were no job development agencies that would provide job placement or any kind of assistance in developing job skills. Slaves were not educated, so what possibility did they have, of obtaining employment from individuals who most likely did not think highly of them in the first place? So, in what way could Blacks live or "survive" within the American system?

Compare the situation of the freed former slaves to that of a dog which has resided with a family since its birth. At a certain age, the family releases the dog from the household. How will the dog now survive within an environment of which it has no understanding and for which it has no training that will enable it to survive? Most likely, the dog will engage in behaviors that are destructive—in human terms, "immoral or unlawful"—in the name of survival. I say in human terms because the dog cannot really know about the law and morality. Now, in no way am I comparing us as a people to dogs or anything like that. The *situation*, however, is similar. We were treated like dogs, released, and set free just like unwanted animals the household no longer had any use for.

I use this comparison to illustrate the way we were thrown into a system of which we had no understanding. Given this heritage, when mistakes are made and wrong paths are taken, where does the real blame belong? The notion of understanding life and understanding how to make it within the American system was not (and is still not) an easy task. Some may argue that there are many who have made it. But where would those individuals be without the guidance, backing, assistance, and education they received along the way? Not everyone has a stable household, educational support, or model upbringing. I am not suggesting that making it only consists of being born with a silver spoon, nor does a silver spoon guarantee making it. However, digging your way up from the bottom is much harder than having more money, guidance, and/or opportunity. So what kind of education do you expect a child to get if he or she is malnourished to where the focus is on eating as opposed to figuring out a plan to become successful within the United

States system? Many who grow up in such conditions will do what is needed in life, and that is *survive.*

Another metaphor that expresses what it is like to survive in the aftermath of slavery is that of climbing a mountain. When climbing a mountain, there are a number of variables that dictate whether the attempt will be successful or not. The climber needs ropes, physical supports, education on how to climb the mountain, and other tools to successfully climb a mountain. Each time you reach the top of the mountain, there is another mountain to climb, and then another, and so on. I equate the mountain to life. Each additional mountain represents different obstacles that we must face as we climb within life.

But imagine climbing that same mountain without rope or support, education or aid. Think of how much more difficult climbing that mountain would be without the tools needed to elevate you to the next level. In other words, consider how much more difficult life would be without aid, support, and understanding. This is how it was when we were "freed" from slavery. Without any understanding of how to climb a mountain, we still had to make our way by any means deemed fit if we were to survive. When our people were released from the obligation of slavery, what ropes, supports, or aids were available to ensure an easier or even a clear path within mainstream America? The answer is none. As a result, many of us had to choose paths within life without any guidance or clear sense of direction, leading to a survival mentality.

Thus, the path of survival has now become the common path or blueprint for most Black families. The path is seldom questioned because it has always been done this way. But if we continue to do things the way they have always been done, how then can we "overcome," as the song proclaims we should? Have we arrived at our destination? Are the majority of Blacks living well, well off economically and developed educationally as much as other cultures, or are we still stuck in the same old stories, scripts, and movies with no other change than different settings and/or backgrounds?

Chapter Three

Back to Basics

"We are confused out here; I mean the typical family with a mom and dad is extinct in the Black community. I bet out of ten niggas, only one or two of you grow up with a mom and dad in the same house."

-Mass Man "Black Relationships"

When I was younger, there were values that provided a structure for governing the family and the community. At some point, those values changed, and not for the better. What happened and when did the shift take place? There are some that say rap music and other influences from mass culture are to blame. In some respects, that is true because the subliminal messages and imagery from popular music, video games, news media, and movies has a profound effect on shaping the mind. What is certain though, is that the basis, origin, and foundation of the family have been lost.

I reiterate my earlier comments that the lack of or loss of fathers within the household hugely affects family structure. I am not saying that it is impossible for a mother to breed success; however, in working with youth, I have found that many young people are angry and outraged, yet have no viable means to channel that anger. In my experience, this outraged anger is more apparent in boys. Not in all cases but a true man is more so able to calm a boy better than a woman can. Women cannot fully understand how to raise a boy to become a man so therefore there is a different bond and relationship with boys and men.

When a man has not had a strong man or male role model to guide him through childhood and adolescence, it is no wonder that so many grown men act immaturely. Such immaturity is expressed by a lack of responsibility, having multiple babies by different mothers ("baby mommas," as we call it), as well as a refusal to take part in raising their own children. These are individuals who lack any sense of responsibility. By the same token, young girls who lack fathers or other male influences tend to find their lost love in the arms of another man. In many cases, it is the wrong man.

All of this illustrates some of our problems and where we need to re-establish basic values, such as parenting skills. Whether there is a man at home or not, there is still a basic need to exemplify parenting skills. Before elaborating further on this theme, I would like to praise parents, single mothers in particular, who are taking care of their responsibilities. I know that the task is tough and hard, but in many cases, without you, your children would have nothing. I would also like to praise fathers, the real men who take care of their responsibilities as a man. The point I want to make is that regardless of the situation, parent(s) need to establish basics.

The definition of "basic" is: "pertaining to, or forming a base; fundamental: a basic principle; the basic ingredient."[3] Unfortunately, nowadays we seem to have lost these basic values of child rearing and parenting. When I was growing up, I was taught to respect my elders as well as to respect the boundaries of authority. As I work with children, currently I see that there is a huge lack of respect for elders and authority figures. Working within a public school, I observe how parents often defend the behaviors of their children. It is much easier to blame others for what you (the parent) have not done to control the behaviors of your child than to take responsibility yourself. I also see parents who think it is the school's job to appropriately address the behaviors of their child during school hours. I once had a co-worker who summed it up by saying parents often seem to feel that once they drop off their child at school, they have no responsibility for that child until he or she returns home. They push their child into school stating, "It's your turn, my shift is done." Their expectation, in other words, is that for the next six to seven hours, it is the responsibility of the school to address whatever deep-rooted issues the child has brought from home. What kind of thinking is it when a parent feels as though discipline and structure should be the main purpose of the school? I often tell parents that there is no program or service that can help change a child's behavior if the child is irrational or does not want to follow any directives of authority. In most cases, if respect for authority is not instilled at home, no one can alter a child's irrational and uncontrollable behaviors.

Again, this goes back to basics. Provide the discipline and lay the groundwork needed to govern your child from the beginning, so that any problems which arise later in life can be addressed or, better yet, prevented. What needs to change as well is the understanding of what it means to be a parent, the basic definition. Becoming a parent means taking ownership of the situation and realizing that sacrifices have to be made for your children's sake. All too often, basic parenting skills are lost in the process. If a parent is always negative to their child, how does that affect the child's view of the world? What attitude does the child adopt? I have witnessed parents curse, belittle, and degrade their children. What reason can a parent give for cursing at their children? I have seen mothers tell their child that he will never amount to anything in life or will turn out just like his father, a father who chose the wrong path in life and ended up in prison. Now tell me, how can a child take away anything positive from that? And when the child comes to school angry as a result of such talk, who does the blame fall on? If this same child then ends up in prison later in life, do not be surprised.

Some things should be understood as "Parenting 101." For those unfamiliar with the term "101", it is a designation used in college courses to indicate an introductory-level course. "101" indicates that here you will be taught the basics, the things that come first. When entering college, students begin by taking the 100-level classes first. This is a way to assist in the transition from high school to college before the student takes on more difficult and more advanced classes. The 100-level classes assist students in developing the skills that they will need to succeed in college. Parents too, need some 100-level basic instruction in developing the skills they will need to succeed in raising healthy and happy children. They need 100-level courses on how to parent, how to discipline, how to sacrifice, how to nurture, how to communicate, specific dos and don'ts of parenting, and so on. Advanced courses should come with the advancement of the child. In short, effective parenting skills do not happen automatically for many because a child is born. There are some things that parents simply have to learn, including a basic understanding of what it means to be a parent.

Moving on to address some specific topics, I understand that parents want to provide the best for their children. I get that. But when has it become necessary for a child to receive all kinds of expensive clothing and gadgets simply for being alive? Children who are failing in school receive a new pair of Jordan, LeBron, Kevin Durant sneakers, and other expensive gifts. And younger children have access to far too much technology. I see parents who purchase expensive cell phones, iPads, iPods, and big-screen televisions for eight- and nine year-old kids. Now, what logic or sense does that make? Children are consumed with video games that are rated "mature" which indicate that the game is intended for those who are mature. The content of these games consists of robbery, shooting guns, killings, and cursing. I also see that our notions of privacy have changed due to social media. Children that I work with often suggest that we become Facebook friends or ask if I have a Myspace account (when popular). Is it just me or do other responsible adults think that there is something wrong with young people having accounts on social media where adults can have access to them?

Another area that concerns me is the way that entertainment is pushed into children's lives. Cable television has become an essential part of American way of living; but cable has an array of channels that include programming which are inappropriate for children. I once worked with a family where one of the children mentioned that one of the movies he liked was *Baby Boy*. *Baby Boy*, wow! The kid was in elementary school. Think about the movie: the weed smoking, murder, and the explicit sex scene before she cooked the tacos. As a parent, you should not want to expose your children to what is meant only for adults. Life should be lived in stages. By the same token, I also object to allowing young ladies to wear make-up at a very early age. This sends the wrong message. Plus, the maintenance required to achieve such a look is not the job of an elementary school age girl. And after make-up is introduced, what is the next step? Parents, please, let your children live their life in stages.

Parents need to understand how to parent, how to cultivate their children's development, and they should be ready to learn skills in any other areas that will benefit the child. Parents need to set boundaries for themselves and their children. Children need to develop in stages. There is no reason to engage children in topics suitable only for adults. Parents, when children are around you, you should know that they are listening. They may appear to be preoccupied with their own activities and concerns, but they are also listening to your conversations. When you are talking to friends in person or over the phone and your children are present, please remember that they are also observant.

Anyone with children also needs to realize how much they want your attention. If you are not giving them the attention that they want, children will make you aware of their need in undesirable ways. The girl without her father, for example, will get her attention from the wolves outside the home. There are men who prey on young girls like this solely to take away the girl's innocence. Men, such as these, are like starving lions that smell the blood of the defenseless deer, and the deer does not have a chance or any means of defense. The bait of attraction and attention holds too powerful a pull. In fact, attraction often is not always the factor that achieves the goal. I have had many discussions with women who told me that they do not even know why they gave up their innocence the first time to the guy that they did. Why is that? That deer did not have a chance. I do not believe that anyone who has lost their innocence has been taken in by a wolf or have not been desired; however, in most cases the individual who provides a young girl with attention is able to suck her in. I know there are many people who encounter their "first" later in life and then say to themselves, "Lord, what was I thinking?" This is just one example of how lack of attention breeds seeking attention in unhealthy ways.

As parents, there needs to be an understanding that your children will seek attention by any means necessary, whether the attention is positive or negative. In many instances, children who long for attention will perceive even negative attention as a positive. This is exemplified in the documentary *Crips and Bloods: Made in America*[4], which covers the Bloods and Crips gangs. The documentary shows just how crucial attention can be in a young person's life. In the film, one gang member shared how an O.G. (Original Gangster) took him in, clothed and fed him for a month. Essentially, the person looked out for him when no one else had. Thus, when trouble arose, he felt obligated to show loyalty by engaging in gangbanging that comes with the gang lifestyle. So parents please understand that a child who does not receive proper attention or guidance at home can be sought out as prey by undesirable influences. And thus knowledge, wisdom, understanding, and planning can assist in development of our youth to become productive citizens in society.

Chapter Four

The Curse

"When you control a man's thinking you do not have to worry about his actions. He will find his proper place and will stay in it. You do not need to send him to the back door. He will go without being told."[1]

-Carter G. Woodson. *The Mis-Education of a Negro*

We are cursed in so many ways and there are so many people who seem not to understand this fact of life or acknowledge the need for a cure. Think about it. How is it that we so often see repeated negative patterns within a particular family? For example, take a family where the mother or father, aunts, uncles, and all other family members have ended up in prison. Then, at some point in life, their children end up in prison. Or we see a family with a long history of having children at a young age. Having children too young causes an array of problems, the greatest of which are economics. Money, or rather the lack thereof, lies at the root of these problems. Equally important, young people do not know who they are or where they are going. Because of this, they lack parenting skills and understanding of how to guide or discipline their children.

When we see these kinds of negative family patterns that continue on from generation to generation, it is no exaggeration to call them a curse. A curse is defined as: "a solemn utterance to invoke a supernatural power to inflict harm or punishment on someone or something."[2] The curse that I speak about so often within these pages is one that we need to acknowledge and make the focus of our attention: it is a family curse.

If we are to provide a cure for this curse, we must first understand its psychological aspects and the way the effects of this curse have been passed down from generation to generation. A family curse is a cycle that continues to perpetuate itself. It is like a circle that ends up back where it starts.

Have you ever wondered why we as Black folks tend to use physical discipline rather than other forms of punishment when it comes to our kids? Take a look at how we were disciplined, at how our mothers and fathers were disciplined, and our grandparents. In my case, my great grandparents, or their parents, were disciplined by physical forms of punishment:

whipping, lashes, or lynching. We have internalized the form of discipline taught to us by the slave master, and therefore assume that is what we are supposed to do. I wonder whether this physical discipline is just another way to escape the anger, oppression, and suppression we feel as a people by inflicting physical force on others in turn.

I would like to slip in just one suggestion about the curse that I think is important to discuss, though I do not want to elaborate or go into great detail. Like our behaviors, the type of foods that we as a people tend to consume was also passed down from generation to generation. We eat things like pig knuckles, pig feet, chitterlings, hog maws, fat back, chicken gizzards, and so on. As a child, I did not understand how someone could enjoy the taste of chitterlings. I still do not understand it. I was first introduced to chitterlings by my mother's friend, who woke me up one morning with the smell of chitterlings he was cooking downstairs. The whole house smelled like manure. Chitterlings are the intestines of the pig. If you have studied anatomy, you know that the intestines are where the waste is stored. For the life of me, I cannot understand how anyone can enjoy food with the smell, taste, and residue of manure. Now, where did the taste for these foods come from?

These foods were deemed dirty, filthy animal scraps which the slave masters did not want. The slaves had no choice but to eat the scraps that were thrown their way, and so these kinds of foods became traditional recipes that were passed down in Black families.

But these kinds of foods that originally came from the scraps thrown to us as slaves are not good for us. Nevertheless, being the innovators that we are, we took the worst of the worst that had been thrown our way and made something out of nothing. We took something negative and made it into a positive for ourselves. It was either that or starve. So we are accustomed to take the worst of things and make them into something better for ourselves, to take a negative and turn it into a positive.

Another illustration of taking something bad appearing good is the word "nigger," which was a label with overwhelmingly negative connotations. But what did we do with that word? We turned it into "negro" or "nigga." I will not profess to know what positive derived out of "negro," but "nigga" is used in many ways among Blacks. More educated Blacks typically avoid using the word. Tupac broke down the word nigga turning it to a positive. He suggested that those that use the term, to suggest to not lack in ignorance to accomplish goals. Thus, he turned a negative into a positive.

Though foods such as chitterlings are still consumed and considered by most people within the Black community something positive and delicious, they remain a negative: they are harmful to your health. Health concerns such as obesity, high blood pressure, clogged arteries, and the consumption of slave foods are all inter-related. We need to break the curse of consuming such unhealthy foods so the next generation will not have to endure the curse of ill health.

Curse in other forms

A neighbor of mine, an old-school gentleman, shared some-thing with me that was profound. I told him that I was working, but my passion was to finish this book, which I had been working on for some time now. He asked what I was writing about and I shared that I was writing about what is going on with us as Black people. I threw out some topics that I had thought of and told him what I wanted to do. Then the gentlemen shared something with me that sparked an idea which I knew I could elaborate on and develop if I put more thought into what he had shared. As soon as he said it, I was completely taken with the idea and immediately told him that I was going to use what he had just said. He continued to dig deep as we talked further. As my blood boiled and my passion began to rise, I had to disconnect from the topic, otherwise I would be there talking for hours. As my car heated up, I jumped inside, driving away, trying not to be late for that J-O-B (just over broke).

For the next two days, I thought about how I was going to compose the information. As ideas began to formulate, the next day on my way to the J-O-B, it hit me how I was going to elaborate on what the gentlemen had shared with me. And what were the words that sparked my passion? "No slave will ever have ownership in a land which is already owned by its masters." (Though I would like to give credit to the author of that quote, I was not able to find the source). Now, what does this saying mean? To me, it means that though we have made some progress, there is only a certain level to which we can aspire. We are sectioned off by barriers that defend society at large against change.

To explain what I mean about how "we" are sectioned off, I will use the game of Othello as an example. In Othello, the object of the game is for one player's color to exert dominance over the other. There are only two colors in Othello: black and white. The board is represented by green. Some with a deep analytical mind would suggest that the green represents the earth, the inter-changeable black and white pieces represent people, and that the object of the game is to see who will dominate the earth. The game is won by which ever color dominates in number.

Now, how is it played? Four pieces are set up in the middle of the board. The two opposing colors are lined up across from one another both vertically so that pieces of the same color face one another in the blocks that are diagonal to one another, making a crisscross of the same colors illustrating an X. Each playing piece is two-sided, and there are rules that govern when a piece is flipped over to the opposite color. When playing, each player attempts to gain the advantage by placing a playing piece of their color in a space next to their opponent's piece, which will force the opposite player to turn over their playing piece so that it shows the color of the person making the move. This is done by sandwiching the pieces. For example, if I have one black chip and there are five white chips underneath, I can place a black chip at the end of the white pieces and turn all five of the white chips black. So at that moment, the color black is dominating. Color manipulation continues throughout the course of the game until the end.

Those who have never played the game may ask, what is the overall advantage of color domination? Whenever I play, I try to control the corners and the borders. If I control the corners, then I can control the manipulation of colors from left to right, as well as in the middle, as long as they are connected to the corner pieces. There are four corners within the game. So the object is control, control, control. But what if the game started with all four corners already controlled? In that scenario, no matter how hard you play, winning is basically impossible, or extremely difficult at the least. "Unfair advantage" is what I call it. So in order to get an advantage, the pieces without corner control have to fight, fight, fight, and fight just to have a shot at winning, thus our inception into the United States system.

Fighting does not necessarily mean violence, such as the use of guns, killing, or death, although those are the means employed in most revolutionary fights in order to gain a shot at winning. But who is behind this negativity (violence) in the service of revolution? The oppressed, who simply want to make a change in their status (poor people who "do not matter" in society at large), or those who oppress the poor? When you are poor in this society, you do not matter unless you do something that matters. For example, if I start a fight and hit someone, should I be mad or upset when the defendant strikes back? In other words, violence is the means most often employed when a revolution is started in the sense of fighting back.

The Urban Dictionary defines rebel as "a person who stands up for their own personal opinions despite what anyone else says."[1] A true rebel stands up for what they believe is right, not against what's perceived as right. If someone causes harm to you or your family, why shouldn't you rebel against them? But if you rebel, the corner control— otherwise known as "the law"—it will be perceived that you are doing wrong in fighting for fairness and equality. Examples of this are Dr. Martin Luther King Jr, Malcom X, The Black Panthers, and other organizations strive for the betterment of all people.

If self-defense in a revolutionary context is considered wrong, then what would righteous self-defense look like? Dr. Martin Luther King's nonviolent approach only resulted in more violence against people that were nonviolent. But when violence and injustice spiral out of control, what should be done? Should people allow the harm and destruction to continue? Take, for example, the riots in Los Angeles following the verdict against Rodney King, which showed how such disparity in justice leads to a situation that boils out of control. While in no way do I agree with burning and destroying your own community, but yet I understand it. I understand why it happened, and I agree that a change needed to occur. And though I do not agree with those who destroyed their own community, I understand that the pot had boiled over with injustice and frustration. The Rodney King trial and the verdict that followed was first of all a joke when you consider the way it was handled and resolved. It clearly depicted that we do not matter. *NOT GUILTY!!* How? In the face of videotaped proof and evidence, how was such a verdict even possible? Now tell me this, think of how different things would have been had the police been Black and Rodney King been White?

Chapter Five

The Drug Dealer

"Thought about trapping just to get a couple bucks/ but the money that I make doesn't equate the time I spend in cuffs."

-Mass Man, Somewhere In This World

Many people have entered the game of drug dealing. Some have made a great deal of money, while others have chased the dream only to find themselves in a position of either death, prison, or living life in a crippled state. This crippled state comes through the war of gunshots or getting high on your own supply. Yes, drug dealers have the ability to become addicted to the very product they sell. There are countless documented stories that explain the rise and fall of those who have played the game of drug dealing. There are a number of celebrated high profile ex-drug dealers such as Rayford Edmonds and a larger number of Rayford "Deadmen" who have chased the American Dream through drug dealing. I use the name Rayford "Deadmen" as a way to cover the number of dead men that have lost their lives within the drug game. Rayford Edmonds was a legendary, iconic figure who made a huge amount of money by selling drugs during the late 80's and 90's. However, Rayford's life will end behind bars because of his success of being a drug dealer.

His story (Rayford Edward) is well documented, as there are a number of documentaries that Blacks glorify or use as a tool for knowledge. There was AZ, Rich Porter, and Alpo, as well as Guy Fisher, Nicky Barnes, Freeway Rick Ross, and countless others. To me, all the stories basically end the same. Most of these men rode the wheels until the wheels fell off of their situation. The ending result was that the individuals either lived (or are still living) in jail or are deceased. If this is the case, why are there still other individuals that want to pattern their lives in the same manner? As a drug dealer, there are only a few options, death, prison, or addiction.

Though a drug dealer is criticized for the behaviors and actions of the illegal activity that destroys many lives, I have to be mindful not to be so quick to judge. I cannot honestly say that the allure of money would not have enticed me to want to change my status in the past, which was under the poverty level. To think about it, who really wants to live under the poverty level? Though I was able to evade the patterns and trappings of a specific life, I cannot say that I would not have done so if there were not different situations and factors that changed my life. Mentality, chance, and opportunity are things that one cannot take for granted. As we watch the news and witness people getting locked up, we are quick to judge the individuals at the bottom, because they are being publicized in the media. If the ones pulling the strings at the top of the drug game were cut off, then there would not be high-level crimes at the bottom. However, drugs have become an enormous money producer for individual communities, businesses, prisons, programs, and most importantly, America.

Now with the private companies making money hand over fist with profit for prison, they make money even when a drug dealer is not selling drugs. It is like the gift that keeps on giving. Christmas could be all year round. The drug game has been in existence for so long that it has become quite normal in a sense that people, at least in the poor communities, actually live life around it. There are always more deals, murders, imprisonments, and deaths with no real ending. One thing that I do not understand is that drugs have been a major part of American society for at least twenty years, even though we know it is longer. However within that time, there have been many drug related arrests, where large amounts of money have been consumed. One thing that is not known to the general public is that with the large amounts of money that has been confiscated, where does all of the money go? How is it spent? Who gets it?

My thought is if the money comes from the "hood" (poor communities); why not have the money returned to the hood for the benefit of the hood? At the present moment during the current war on drugs, I would say that at the least fifty million dollars has been confiscated. Some say bad money turned good is always a blessing. But I guess it is only a blessing for those that have the access to these blessings.

Chapter Six

Knowledge of Self

"How do you keep information away from a Black person? Put it in a book." (Anonymous) **"Education is the passport to the future, for tomorrow. The future belongs to those who prepare for it today."**[1] - Malcolm X

If hiding information from Black people can be done by wedging it in a book, what does that say about us? With this connotation, what does it mean for Blacks? It is simple; we are laughed at because "we" are too dumb to seek and find information within a book or to pick up a book to read. In working with the youth, I find that there are many of our children that are inefficient in reading. Parents tell me that their children are doing poorly in reading and math. I ask them how much does their child read. Most of the parents will suggest that there is no reading being done at home. Now why is that? It is proven that the more you read, the more reading skills will improve. Reading is the gateway to opening the mind and exploring new possibilities. I once heard somewhere, maybe on television, about a man who did not learn how to read until he was in prison, so could there be a correlation between prison and not reading?

When I first begin working with families and children within their homes, I inquire how much television is being watched and how much time is dedicated to playing video games. I am blown away of the lack of time dedicated in reading compared to the amount of time watching the idiot box (the television) or playing video games. In a lot of cases, there is no reading taking place. Over the summer, in a large number of the families I have worked with, not one book has been read by their child. Why is that? This is the reason that I encourage parents to implement at least thirty minutes a day for each child to read. If you think about it, thirty minutes is a drop in a bucket compared to the amount of time a child spends watching television, playing video games, or engaging in some other form of entertainment.

Since the beginning of our inception from Africa, the purpose of not being educated was to keep us ignorant, deaf, dumb, and blind. Webster Dictionary defines ignorance as "the state or fact of being ignorant : lack of knowledge, education, or awareness"[2]. Deaf means to lack the ability to hear, which enables one not to understand. Dumb is classified as not being smart enough to figure things out. The term blind, in this case, is the ability to not see what is going on, even when it is in front of you (the logic and reasoning skills to see behind the mask or masked illusions). One must adopt and train themselves to think on a higher level. We must think about things that we are conditionally distracted by, because these distractions create a lack of knowledge and a loss of focus on what is going on with education, lack of Black production, and so many other variables that affect us as Blacks. Along with the distractions, understand the poison that is being fixated in our minds. Television, music, news, music videos, movies, etc., are all measures of mind control.

These are good ways to distract the public, while brainwashing minds in order to control people. Music is a huge tool within the Black community. Does anyone ever try to understand why there are not any uplifting rap songs on the radio now? Why is that? When I was younger, I learned through inspiration and uplifting rap that talked about the struggle and "fighting the power". Presently, rap has become a vehicle to encourage money, money, and more money. Rappers are not developing messages to inspire but the model fantasies of partying and money. Correction, the industry that controls radio, air play, and promotion does not encourage positivity for us that listen to rap. So rap has become a form of monopoly where those that inspire are locked out. And the industry that is in control does not care of the progression of Blacks, but concerned about the money while causing destruction and confusion.

As I am discussing rappers and rap music, I want to address a topic that I find interesting. In current rap music, we have the braggadious rappers who brag about their houses, cars, and all the money that they foolishly throw away. One rapper even suggests that he has a mortgage around his neck. The average fan that buys this music will most likely never obtain what it is that the rappers are talking about. Therefore, the rappers are bragging in the face of the people, in a sense. But as the rapper continues to make money and brag about possessions, he/she will ask for support. How so? I mean, are the rappers/entertainers supporting the neighborhoods and places in which they come from? *Hmmm.*

In my opinion, it is no coincidence that our music does not produce positivity when the aim for us is to be left behind. As slaves, we were not allowed to educate our minds. Why is that? If I become educated, I become more aware that I have options. A slave that became educated understood that he/she was more than a slave and that there were more options outside of slavery. Education allows me to understand that working at McDonald's is not an option. Thus, there is a profound understanding that educating the mind is a powerful thing. Even Lil' Wayne, a popular rapper, suggested to having read the dictionary to expand on his vocabulary in writing raps. In order to get ahead within the rap game, Lil' Wayne wanted to gain more understanding and more knowledge. Whether it is through formal education or informal education, education and knowledge are forever powerful in understanding what is going on within society.

When I speak of an understanding about what is going on in society, I am not talking about the news that develops untold truths. As I previously stated, history is breaking down as "history". It is the interpretation of something, information that the person wants you to believe. However, education is so powerful that when an individual or organization has educated the people beyond average understanding, that individual or organization has to be eliminated, well in the content of being Black. For example, Martin Luther King, Malcolm X, and the Black Panther organization were individuals or an organization that strived for social change and equality. In the fight and struggle, Martin Luther King and Malcolm X were assassinated. In the case of the Black Panther organization, there were many that lost their lives as well. As it is well documented, the government's top aim was to destroy the Panthers because of their own agenda. The main reason for the tragic loss is that the leaders were intelligent, insightful, and had people to think above what was going on in society. The Panthers and many other Black intellects also exposed reality of the lies that have brainwashed people within the American system.

What was so wrong with speaking out for change and having a fair share of the American pie? Why does equality for all spoken by our strong Black leaders have to equate to death? Additionally, why does speaking about injustice and promoting change have to lead to individuals losing their lives? Think about it, or better yet, look around you. Put the pieces of the puzzle together. Understand that in the past, our history had been taken away from us so that we could not know about ourselves, culture, and our many contributions to society. As my cousin Mass Man says in his song "Some Where In The World", "jail is another place where all the violence is/, poverty in the streets come from policies of our politics/ man know thy self/ only way to get up out of this/ school of hard knocks my whole block gotta scholarship."

Understand that the overall plan was for Blacks not to obtain education, an informed mind, or knowledge of self. When we do not read or consume our minds with the wrong information, it is easy to forget about our Black struggle. When we continue to not seek and learn our history, when we continue to not get our education, we are conspiring with the plan that was created for us. At the same time, as we lack in development, we spit in the faces of our ancestors, who have fought for change that would allow us to have a better life to this day. So are we fighting for development and change in support of our ancestors or have we lacked in support by spitting in their faces?

Chapter Seven

Slavery vs. Prison

"I'm beginning to believe that U.S.A. stands for the Underprivileged Slaves of America."[1]

Slavery vs. Prison, what is the difference? Before the abolishment of slavery, the act of slavery was first the law. Slavery was shackles, chains, and bars. Being shipped from your homeland to a place that you did not want to be, having to live doing work or things that you did not want to do. In the end, what did all slaves want? Freedom. During slavery, there was rebellion, fighting, and a large number of deaths/murders. When you did not conform or resisted authority, there were influences that would force you to conform against your will.

The influence to conform is similar to the movie *State Property*. In the movie, rapper/actor Beanie Sigel extorted other drug dealers for a piece of their business, using the motto "get down or lay down." This meant that the person either had to conform to his power and program or face death. If you think about it, the institution of slavery first implemented this same system of "get down or lay down." Another example of this method that clearly depicts how we were forced into becoming state property was told in the movie *Roots*. Kunta Kinte was the African slave who fought and rebelled against slavery until he could no longer fight the power that controlled him. When the slave owners whipped Kunta and asked him his name, he would fight and fight. Kunta Kinte did not want to adopt the name "Toby," the name in which his master had provided for him. Of course, we all know how the story unfolded. Kunta eventually could not withstand the pain of the lashes that would have eventually killed him had he not confirmed to the system pressed upon him by his master.

Although he ultimately adopted the name Toby, he continued to rebel by running away from the plantation. As a result, the punishment of "get down or lay down" became more severe with Toby's foot being amputated in order to keep Toby confined to the plantation.

As stated previously, all slaves wanted freedom. To be free from performing duties that were forced on us, being raped, whipped, controlled, and murdered. All slaves wanted to be free from the mental and physical control of another human being. However, when freed, we were free to what?

There are certain elements of prison that are similar to slavery. Just like slavery, the police act as the law. There are shackles, chains, and bars. You are also shipped from your home or homeland to a place where you do not want to be. If you do not follow the rules, you are forced to submit. There are various tactics that can be used to make you change your way of thinking. You will also have to do things that you do not want to do. In prison, you really do not have the capacity to make money and/or earn a living. If you do work, I believe that the money earned could be classified as slave wages.

What needs to be understood is that our origin into the American system and instructions on how to live was formulated in prison by way of slavery. Therefore, it is fair to say that America wanted Blacks to be hindered and controlled by a prison lifestyle. Our names and history were stripped away during slavery, just like it is in modern day prison. When you go to jail, your name is stripped away, and you become nothing but a number. Just as the name Toby and other names were forced onto slaves, the numbers are forced onto inmates while in prison.

When we look at statistics of the vast number of Blacks who are incarcerated compared to the other ethnic groups, why is it that more Blacks are in prison than any other race? Now I base this off of the percentage of race and population in which Blacks are at the top. Most prison populations are formed by ethnic groups that are the poorest according to economic standards. Secondly, what I cannot understand is if we as Blacks produce more children at a higher rate for many generations, how is the Black race still considered the "minority"? The word "minority" acts as a label to classify a group as less than who are not good enough. If something is minor or less than, would that thing be equal to the whole?

Adversely, one thought that comes to mind about the large, present number of imprisoned Blacks is that it was (and still is) the plan within the system for us. If one takes a close look at what is going on, there can be a correlation found between slavery and how it relates to society in 2015. In 2015, the old form of slavery cannot exist, such as being confined to a plantation, work without pay, and to be beaten, raped, or killed without fighting back. We have become too strong mentally where we would fight back against the old form of slavery, as Nat Turner did, but we would fight back in the new form of slavery? We would not conform to the terms and conditions set up by the system of slavery because our mindset is different. Although we cannot be shackled in the same manner, we have become shackled in various other ways within society. Case in point: college, lack of jobs, reduced education, less opportunities, subliminal mind control to name just a few invisible shackles.

Also, we have become more humane as a nation than the individuals that lived back in the days of slavery, so therefore the methods used in times of slavery cease to exist. In taking a closer look into modern day society, the stage is still set for slavery. The only difference is that the terms, conditions, and laws have been changed. And with these changes, we too must change in our actions and way of thinking in order to devise a more stabilized plan to avoid the masters' plan.

The 13th Amendment

The amendment reads "Neither slavery nor involuntary servitude *except as a punishment for crime* whereof the party shall have been duly convicted shall exist within the United States, or any place subject to their jurisdiction" (emphasis mine).[2]

The 13th amendment suggests that slavery is still in full operation, due to the terms and documentation within it. Since the abolishment of slavery, we cannot be enslaved against our own will. The inhumane acts, treatment, deprivation, disparity, destruction, psychological derogation, and other actions are only translated to slavery in a more modernized manner. The trick that has been presented is that slavery has ended. No, we do not have to reside on the plantation being shackled or chained, but is that not prison? No, we will not get whipped if we do not follow rules of the individuals that would be considered masters. If slavery was abolished, then there should be an end to it without exceptions.

In the 13th amendment, there was an organized plot that released us from slavery in one way but taken as slaves in another way, thus various forms of prison. As slavery ended, it appeared as if we were free; however to be placed in prison stripped away of our rights, thus placing us back into slavery. In 1865, slavery was "supposedly" ended. I say "supposedly" because in 2015, there are still Blacks that feel as though they are not free, very much trapped and enslaved. When Blacks were set free from the plantation, the plan was to enslave Blacks through prison. *"Prisoners are, by mandate of the United States Constitution, slaves." -Rev Murphy Davis.*[3]

It was understood that a Black man or woman could be legally enslaved by way of prison. After slavery ended, who would provide that cheap labor profit in which no one else would do? Thus, prison workers produced cheap labor profit. Slavery plus work equals dollars and with slavery being abolished, more strategized methods had to be implemented to keep the money rolling. This means that the powers that be were not going to allow all of that money to be lost, therefore slavery would continue by way of prison.

"Slavery is fundamentally an economic phenomenon. Throughout history, slavery has existed where it has been economically worthwhile to those in power. The principal example in modern times is the U.S. South. Nearly 4 million slaves with a market value of close to $4 billion lived in the U.S. just before the Civil War." -Jenny B. Wahl[4]

The Civil War began in 1861 and the estimated profit for slavery was four billion dollars before 1861. Slavery, or the control of slaves, ended in 1865 with the Emancipation Proclamation passed by former President Abraham Lincoln. With that amount of legalized profit, how could the oppressors afford to lose all of that money? They could not and would not. The ending of slavery suggested that money would be lost, plus there was no one to do the slave work. Therefore, systems had to be placed or redesigned within the contents of the law, in order to continue ruling and controlling the Black slaves that were now free.

According to Wikipedia, the free encyclopedia, there is a term called "convict leasing" that replaced legalized slavery. Convict leasing is a system of penal labor practiced in the southern United States, beginning with the emancipation of slaves at the end of the Civil War in 1865, peaking around 1880 and ending in Alabama, in 1928. The purpose of the system was to enslave Blacks to provide prison labor to private parties, such as plantation owners and corporations. The article also suggests that, "African Americans, due to vigorous and selective enforcement of laws and discriminatory sentencing, made up the vast majority."[5]

To support other evidence, Douglas Blackmon writes in *The Re-Enslavement of Black Americans from the Civil War to World War II*: It was a form of bondage distinctly different from that of the South in that for most men, and the relatively few women drawn in, this slavery did not last a lifetime and did not automatically extend from one generation to the next. But it was nonetheless slavery – a system in which armies of **free men, guilty of no crimes and entitled by law to freedom**, were compelled to labor without compensation, were repeatedly bought and sold, and were forced to do the bidding of white masters through the regular application of extraordinary physical coercion.[6]

Though the system was wrong in the oppression of freed Blacks, this system continued to succeed for a number of years because of the legalities within the law. Since the system excelled after the Civil War, it showed that slavery did not end, but took on a different form and appearance. A more camouflaged effect within the confinement of the law, thus the thirteenth amendment. In his book *Slavery and the Penal System* criminologist Thorsten Sellin states that "the sole aim of convict leasing was financial profit to the lessees who exploited the labor of the prisoners to the fullest, and to the government which sold the convicts to the lessees."[7]

Like all good news, word spread in the South about how to control Blacks and how to continue slavery legally. Convict leasing became increasingly "racialized"; it was assumed that blacks were more suitable for hard physical labor on Southern prison farms and on corporate railroad and construction company projects (Lichtenstein, 1996b).[8] However in other areas convict leasing, or better yet convict labor, took on additional forms. In Northern prisons, which had historically been structured around industrial rather than agricultural labor, racially based divisions were sharpened after emancipation as well. African Americans were criminalized for committing Black Code type crimes and often were subject to tougher sentences than those imposed upon whites convicted of similar crimes (Du Bois,1935)[9]. Wikipedia states:

The Black Codes were laws in the United States after the Civil War with the effect of limiting the civil rights and civil liberties of Blacks. These laws had the intent and the effect of restricting Black people's freedom and of compelling them to work in a labor economy based on low wages or debt." Even though the U.S. Constitution originally discriminated against Blacks in both Northern and Southern states had passed discriminatory legislation from the early 19th century, the term "Black Codes" is used most often to refer to legislation passed by Southern states at the end of the Civil War. The laws controlled the labor, migration and other activities of newly-freed slaves.[10]

To elaborate further regarding tricknology again at work and again at its best, more interpretation is needed. "A vagrant or a vagabond is a person, often in poverty, who wanders from place to place without a home, or regular employment or income."[11] So when we discuss freedom (from slavery or the bondage of slavery) what does that really mean? And were we really free? Black codes were and still is a way to keep perceived freed Blacks in line, and in continued bondage of slavery. Freedom in my depiction is free-dom or better yet classified as free the dumb. One had to be dumb to believe that free will, free liberty, free justice, and any other merit of a free world was possible. When one buys a house or car for that matter should the buyer look at the outside only? Should one look at what looks good on the surface to determine the potential to buy? A smart/wise man or woman will take the necessary steps to further investigate the full details needed to have a full understanding of what is really going on. A beautiful home will attract many buyers, but a wise individual will uncover the growing mold in the walls after doing further research. Similar to a wise person discovering the damage up under the hood of a car to determine that the engine will not last. So let us begin to uncover and discover what has happened after the aftermath of free-dom. Many Blacks believed that there was change and opportunity outside of and off the plantation that enslaved them. Once slavery had been perceived to have ended, many remained in the slave like mentally to stay bonded to the only life that they knew. Thus sharecropping was the term used as the now legalized slavery. As there were others that dreamed bigger to think outside of the box of remaining on the plantation, some wanted to venture out to seek work off of the plantation to build and grow in the name of freedom. The law now made it possible for Blacks to be equal and accepted as fee men and women. Jobs and more opportunity was just around the corner, or so we thought. So many would seek to find work in a foreign land from individuals that did not care, like, nor respect the law of free-dom. This is where tricknology strikes once again. The act of freedom was a victory without a victory. Just as many ventured out to seek a better way or a better life, Blacks (freed men and women) were faced with Black codes, **"laws that tried to control freed Black slaves.** Vagrancy laws were included in these codes. Homeless unemployed Black Americans were arrested and fined as vagrants. As the person could not afford the fine, and so was sent to county labor or hired out to a private employer." Thus slavery. In further research of vagrancy laws, it was said that the police arrested people who were suspected of committing a crime. Again that is suspected, not guilty but if I think or say that you did, one is subjected to guilt. This is similar to one having to prove innocence as opposed to having the burden of proof to convict.

So let us review for a second what has been discussed in full understanding. Blacks or yet "freed Blacks" left the plantation looking for a better way and a better life. Blacks looked for work and more opportunity. When this did not occur, under the laws, Blacks can be fined and sent to jail. Now wait, I do not perceive to be the smartest man but if I am fined without employment, then I am sure to go to jail due to not being able to pay the fines. In the content of the law in which Blacks were imprisoned, that meant free work labor on a plantation, the tricknology used within the south. Now this practice was not only limited to those within the south. But do understand that the act or actions spread in all areas where free slave labor was still needed.

Therefore, understand and become aware of the many years where tricknology has and still affects us. Our existence into the United States has been prison (via slavery) and once slavery ended, Blacks were large in number, in regards to the prison population. In 2015, there is still a huge amount of Blacks that are in prison. So I ask, are we truly free or dominated by the master's plan?

Chapter Eight

Voluntary Slavery

"Being a Black man in America isn't easy. The hunt is on, and you're the prey!!!"[1]

-Charles H. Dutton from *Menace to Society*

Sometimes, there are plans and traps set so that we will enslave ourselves. I classify voluntary slavery as the crimes one commits that results in people being locked up and enslaved behind bars. These acts of crimes that are committed suggest that individuals voluntarily place his or herself in the capacity of a loss or deficit in life.

However, not to jump away from the original concepts of understanding the traps that will enslave us, but to better explain this point, think about who controls the drugs being brought into the United States of America. Is it the Black man? Though Blacks do not control the ships, planes, drugs, or guns, we are the ones that endure the brunt of frontline drug dealing. As a result of the massive flood of the uncontrollable substance that is spread amongst the "minorities," individuals are sucked into the voluntary wave of crime. Voluntary is the term used because we all have a choice to engage or not engage in an act of criminal behavior. I understand that some may become involved in the drug trade to feed their families or just themselves.

I am aware that some people may not have received the opportunity as a child to learn the importance of obtaining an education, which will assist one in opening more doors of opportunity than the individual who had not received an education. Nonetheless, one must understand the risk and consequences associated with becoming involved in actions that are against the law. Also, one should have knowledge that with the migration of Africans to America, the definite aim was for the slaves to not become educated. Slaves were to be deaf, dumb, and blind about what was going on within the American system. So, slaves did not believe that there were other opportunities outside of the conditions in which the slaves reside, thus institutionalized thinking.

One must position themselves to educate his or herself in order for the doors of opportunity to open. Because of this, the grounds for enslavement behind bars do not become an end result within one's life because crime is not needed. The slave that becomes educated realizes and understands that slavery (prison or jail) is not an option and does have more opportunities available. Most prisoners that become educated realize that they are better than being a slave, therefore voluntary acts of crime is not an option. Now do understand that slavery is still alive and kicking. Slavery is bad no matter what, but many of us are slaves but do not even know it. Please understand that there are many variations of slavery. Prison is the worst form of slavery, but many are slaves to debt, jobs, mortgages, marriages, etc. Slavery to me is anything that keeps you in bondage when one wants to be free. All in all, one should live life to not volunteer to be a slave behind bars and, again, to not conspire to become part of the masters 'plan.

Chapter Nine

<u>Systems</u>

"The system, orderly function of operation for the supreme benefit for the true people the system was designed for. And when you think of Black, the system is more so derogation, poverty, and trap."

-Charles E. Hill III, M.S.

The definition of the word system can be classified as: orderliness; an ordered manner, one's physiological or psychological constitution.[1] America operates out of many different systems, in all essence for the benefit of the government and/or selected class of people. These systems were set up and an implementation of the laws that never considered Blacks in mind. When the Constitution was written, were there any Blacks at the roundtable? Was there anyone that would oversee the fairness of the laws? The answers are "no", because there was no fairness or equality in mind for a race that did not matter.

The system was created without the thought of fairness or equality for Blacks. However, does the system now suggest fairness and equality? For example, if things are fair, why is it that a law such as affirmative action needs to be implemented for Blacks? An act like this suggests that there is a problem with the hiring of Blacks (and other minorities) on an equal playing field. It implies that the American pie is being dominated and divided so that we cannot eat.

If everything is fair, why do Blacks rank higher in aspects of being incarcerated, having less education, living in poverty, and all other categories of negativity in America?

In what ways did the systems that have been in place for so many generations, and continue to exist, benefit Blacks as a whole? If there is a benefit, then I myself need to become educated on this process.

America is comprised of many systems such as:

1. Education (College/Secondary)

2. School System (Public to Private)

3. Welfare System

4. Taxes

5. Drugs

6. Jail (penal code) System (for adults and juveniles)

7. Banking

8. Military (Armed Forces)

The banking system is important since it is a huge part of the American system. There was a vast amount of money, old money that exists from the slave trade and other business ventures due to the work production of Blacks. Thus, the promise of reparations which we were tricked into believing we would receive. However, Black labor is the cornerstone of operations of the American system.

There is still a large amount of old money generated from the sale of alcohol (during the time when it was illegal). Businesses and corporations have been operating off of the money that had been generated by slave trade and slave labor. However in the end, all of the systems operate for the benefit of one thing: money, money, money. There is nothing wrong with obtaining and receiving money, but the problem occurs when obtaining money turns into greed. Greed is the foundation of what the Native Indians experienced when Christopher Columbus "discovered" America. With greed comes takeover. Greed is the reason why prices become high and unaffordable, well at least to common, everyday people.

One last thing I want to say about banking is that at one time when banks and Wall Street were going under, there was a bailout. I see that the education system, at least in my area and most urban states, are losing money to the point where bankruptcy has been discussed and schools are being closed at alarming rates. So, I wonder, where is the education or human service bailout for the common, everyday people? The answer is, there is none.

Chapter Ten

Black Education

"Jail is another place where all the violence is/, poverty in the streets come from policies of our politics/ man know thy self/ only way to get up out of this/ school of hard knocks my whole block gotta scholarship."
            -Mass Man "Some Where In The World"

Education is defined by the source from Wikipedia as the process by which society deliberately transmits its accumulated knowledge, skills, and values from one generation to another.[1] However, in what sense is education transmitted from one generation to another within the Black community? Also, is the knowledge taught to Blacks from a Black perspective? How has education elevated Black people as a whole, in terms of educational value?

When looking at the statistics of prison, literacy, and academic performance, Black people are either last or close to it. As stated previously, our start into the United States was for us to never be educated. It was unlawful for slaves to be able to read, write, or do math. I talked about the process of being deaf, dumb, and blind in the earlier sections in regards to slavery; however, the process of being death, dumb, and blind still exist to this day.

Most of us do not take the time to understand the methods of tricknology that continue to plague us in the education spectrum. Allow me to explain. We are tricked to believe that all education is fair and equal; education from the schools we attend that are far worst in condition than the schools within the affluent, more developed economic areas. Although I have not traveled to every city in the United States, I understand that the lowest economic areas are predominantly Black. Every state has low income areas, such as ghettos, slums, or hoods, where Blacks reside within the poorest of conditions that breeds future generations of Blacks.

The schools within urban communities have not been remodeled since the building of the schools. Resources are far and few in between. From across the board, city to city, why are the resources for the students in urban communities far less than those in other communities? In some elementary and high school classrooms, I have observed that there were not enough books for all of the students. The breakfast and lunch programs served food that actually suggested low income, with the food appearing to be of low grade, cheap and not edible in observation. If I had a child, my child would not eat this food that lacks nutritional value.

In the educational system for higher learning, I have found that conditions at predominately Black colleges appear to lack the same resources that predominately Caucasian institutions have. In no way am I suggesting that the conditions at every Black college do not match the conditions of non-predominately Black schools. However, there are schools that lack the resources and financial backing as the other institutions. So again, why is it that Blacks receive less?

There is a rap group that declares that schools look like prisons. In my observation of schools within urban communities, I find that the schools do resemble prisons. Is it true that the school and prison systems have correlations with each other? If not, there are factors that link together, depending on the interpretation.

Recent obtained knowledge suggests that the finances and how many prisons are needed in the future are determined by the scores of the fourth-grade literacy test. There is an article entitled, "A $5 Children's Book vs. A $47,000 Jail Cell – Choose One,"[2] provides a breakdown of how test scores are used to predict the cost of future prisons. Basically, if schools fail to educate our children (which have been an on-going curse from generation to generation) there is lack of opportunity upon graduation. And with lack of opportunity means money will be needed from other sources, such as crime. As we can see, the cycle of incarceration continues among Blacks.

Currently, if preparations are being made to provide funding to build more prisons due to lack of educational attainment, then lack of education and prison go hand and hand. With that being said, can students get a fair education when resources are slim, as well as the overall dynamics being different? People need to understand that dynamics, whether in homes or schools, play a huge part in the problems a child may occur in trying to achieve an education.

If the problems at home are vast and conditions do not make for a stable household, then how does a child focus throughout the day? If a child has not eaten the night before and comes to school without receiving breakfast, what level of focus will the teacher receive from the child? If the child is being bullied, harassed, and teased by others while at school, what type of achievement will be obtained here? These are some of the dynamics that play a huge part in the education of a child, which parents, teachers, and others need to be aware of. And these problems do exist. While working at a school with kids that have behavioral problems, I have encountered children that are disruptive within the classroom setting. Once I can identify the problems that the child is having, he or she will share that they have not eaten at the beginning of the school day. Therefore, this child will continue to be a problem until his or her human need is met.

If there is a classroom with overly aggressive and misbehaved students, how can the other students receive what is needed? The schools that have the money will evaluate an aggressive, misbehaved child at a fast pace and determine if the child is not fit for that setting. In the low economic schools, the problems appear to go unsolved. Disruptive students remain in the school setting because there are not enough active alternative solutions for these types of problems. It is only when students become a threat towards others is when something will be done. Therefore, the problems never get resolved, but yet passed along from one year to the next where the problem continues until the students leave that school.

As students continue to be disruptive in school and not become educated, the school system promotes students to the next level although they have not gained or obtained the knowledge needed to move forward. That is like receiving the benefit without earning the benefit. One thing I want Black people to realize and understand is that this is a recipe and is a set-up for failure. A child is passed from one grade to the next, even though this child does not receive what is needed from the previous grade. Yet, the child is still promoted only to be lost in the next higher grade. So when the student graduates, what are the student's options for life?

I have narrowed the options down to a few, basic paths. College is not an option because if the individual did not receive the information from grades 1-12, he/she is not going to magically obtain the necessary knowledge required to succeed in college. Thus, there are about three different options. The first option is to become gainfully employed. Presently, the high school diploma has limitations to what jobs can be obtained and the salary offered. A minimum wage job or a job that pays a little higher than minimum wage is an option for those that want to choose this path. However, the money obtained for a high school graduate tends to be a problem in terms of wanting to live above poverty. I do have to say that there are individuals whom have found a way to live a productive and comfortable lifestyle with only a high school diploma, but the numbers are far and few in between to those whom have not. (Meaning some have worked their way up in the workforce to obtain an affordable lifestyle).

I am not declaring that by only having a high school diploma will there never be an opportunity to make a better life for yourself or family. I am simply stating that the percentage of those that obtain better than low paying jobs with a high school diploma are fewer than those who have completed receiving a higher education.

Option number two is entering into another established system, which is the United States military. There will be more elaboration about this form of system later; however, this is still an area in which education does influence the decision for some to join the armed forces. With limited to no options upon graduating high school, an individual may resort to the military as a way to escape or obtain a better life. I am not suggesting that the military has not provided a good life for some people. Conversely, the act of recruitment is overly extended to the lost and desperate individuals. The enrollment process is packaged so nicely that it becomes very convincing to receive the benefits and amount of money for services. And not everyone is turned on by serving, taking orders, and putting your life on the line to fight in war. Just understand that due to the lack of appropriate educational opportunities, one becomes a target to join the U.S. military.

So if working for a minimum waged job or going to the military is not an option, then how will one survive? If the first two options are not sufficient, then criminal activity is the last option chosen for many to live. As statistics show, the level of crime continues to escalate year after year among Blacks. Whether it is robbing, stealing, drug dealing, or whatever means to make money due to desperation, many people resort to crime. This desperation comes from the lack of options and opportunities for some, while others maybe engaged in that criminal mindset. Therefore, not receiving an education breeds more activity into another system that generates money, which is jail.

So, can you see how promotion without earning it is a complete set-up for Blacks within the school system? All in all, there is not a proven system in place that assists Blacks in attaining proper education across the board. This is evident by the high level of illiteracy, lack of attainment, and the high level of imprisonment that suggest that education is lacking among Blacks. If there is a designated system in place for consistent

African-American achievement, then this system needs to be implemented in the areas where we lack. However in modern times, the money is being taken from the public education for Blacks and being placed in the prison system, suggesting that the path will lead. When it comes to education, it becomes more important to implement more effective systems, resources, and attainment only when money is involved. If you lack money or cannot afford to live in certain areas, children and a class of people are just out of luck.

The message that is clear to me is either the administrators of education do not have a clue about Blacks not receiving a proper education or they do not understand how to educate Blacks. Or is it the fact that the same administrators do not care or conspire to keep Blacks boxed into a plan of destruction, deception, and deprivation? If this problem is going to be tackled and fixed, the problem needs to be addressed from the root. For as long as there has been educational problems, why has it been repeatedly pacified by putting a cheap band aid over the wound? Though the wound continues to resurface, when does the problem properly get addressed? In my opinion, this means that there is an anticipated arrival for you in prison, and the fact is that nothing will change. Most importantly, are you going to fall into the trap or arise above the tricknology that is upon you?

No Child Left Behind

The official No Child Left behind Act is the act geared towards educating students regarding a standardized test. My definition of the act is Blacks being promoted and not left behind though they have not achieved what was needed, as I stated earlier. Associated with this plan and actions is obtaining a full year of work through the summer school program. It amazes me that there continues to be this practice that stands for nothing at all. Yet summer after summer, students sweat in class for a month (18 school days to be exact) and are promoted to the next level, as if within that span of time the students learned all the necessary information. Thus, students are conversely at the same academic level that they were at the end of the school year. So, what is the purpose of summer school? I have observed that credit is granted for completing the program and that credit is promotion, when promotion has not been earned.

Recently, free summer school in some areas has been discontinued and parents are responsible for paying for summer school classes. Due to not desiring to have a high rate of students being retained, students are promoted to the next grade. This again is another way to implement my definition of No Child Left Behind. I was told by a teacher that in order to retain a child, it would take completing at least 44 to 80 pages to retain each student not efficient for promotion. Now with the increased and current demands of paperwork from the school year, can you see how easy it is to implement "No Child Left Behind"?

It is funny how various experiences tie into one another through life. I recall having a conversation with a professor at the end of graduate school. He suggested that I should try my hand at being a teacher. Per his recommendation, he felt as though I would be an excellent teacher. However, being a teacher was never a field in which I wanted to be a part of. Well, not becoming a teacher within a system of teaching I do not believe in. I told the professor that if I were to become a teacher, I would fail students that do not achieve or did not earn the required grades. He shared with me that I would pass the students and I rebutted that I would not. The professor stressed that I would do so because of the pressure from the top (principal, executive administrators, etc.) to pass students even when they do not meet the requirements.

There is no way I would conspire in the destruction of our young boys and girls, these impressionable minds and the future of our race. Not to be misunderstood, I respect the hustle and grind of a teacher. Teachers get a bad reputation when children do not receive their education. People really do not give teachers the credit or admiration for attempting to shape and mold young minds as they face tremendous barriers in making their attempt. Numerous students resist and avoid the assistance/help, but yet the teachers are scrutinized for not being able to perform miracles. There are a number of areas in which teachers go above and beyond the call of duty. I can guarantee that when a teacher was in college, his/her goal was to have a positive effect on children by molding and shaping their minds. I believe that the thought of helping kids excel makes people feel as though they are making a difference.

Once on the job, I believe that most teachers have a different outlook about what is really going on. The first couple of years may be easy; however in time, the burnout and politics of the job becomes a bit much. Please remember that my statements are based on my experiences of observing and communicating with teachers within urban schools.

I know that working with kids can be challenging, yet most schools in the suburbs do not face the overall challenges that urban teachers face. So in understanding that the urban school teachers endure far more challenging conditions, adversely the teachers are paid much less than the suburban school teachers. Urban teachers have to work with less in terms of resources and the lack of a proper disciplinary system. It is hard for a child to be disciplined within urban public schools where the behaviors are not easily changed. For example, in observation of students, I have seen children exhibit terrorizing behavior throughout each school day for an entire school year. Parents are contacted, there are various meetings, and the students are suspended. Yet once the students return to school, the same terroristic behavior resumes. Again, no real discipline or effective actions are implemented to seek effective changes, and if there are effective regulations as a whole, I cannot see them, or at least as far as I can see.

Rules and standards are not enforced at the same rate as suburban schools that have a zero tolerance for defying the rules. The suburban schools have systems in place to change behaviors. If the students are rebellious beyond measure and continuously defy the rules, the next step is to expel the students. The motto I am sure is "one bad apple will not spoil the bunch." I am not suggesting that the suburban schools do not have problems or concerns. However, the behaviors and conditions cannot be compared to the urban schools. Thus, not all conditions apply for all situations. Within urban conditions, there seems to be the same problems year after year which is perceived as the norm.

One of the biggest reasons why the urban schools are notorious for breeding more problems compared to suburban schools is that there are more unstable homes that students come from. I guarantee that there are more students that come from single parent homes, where a man is not present to assist in the productive change of a child. With that point alone, it suggests that the problems are far greater in urban then suburban.

Therefore, in addressing the problems of the urban teacher, there are many hats that teachers must endure. The teachers must first be an educator to the students. The teacher will then take on many tasks outside of the scope or vision that was once conceptualized in college. The teacher becomes a problem solver (to assess attitudes, moods, problems), therapist (whether behavioral or family based), social worker, referee, detective, judge and jury, parent (mom/dad), nurturer, and any other roles needed to benefit the students. Even with all the internal and external factors attached to the job, there is still pressure to perform miracles. Teachers are very much overworked and underpaid. There is also a lack of appreciation from administration, students, parents, etc.

Of course, the classification is not the disrespect from all parents, students, and administrators, but there is a great deal of disrespect across the board. And still with all of the given factors, the urban school teacher still has to work a miracle. What is this miracle that is continuously mentioned? That miracle is the challenge of performing, to wave that magic wand. The miracle for a lot of teachers is to do what other teachers may have not been able to do. That miracle is to educate, educate, educate. Yes, it is to educate the students that rebel and fight against education or may not have yet obtained the skills necessary to be able to learn at their current level. It is to educate students that have not climbed the ladder in previous years of obtaining knowledge, but the next teacher in line has the beautiful task of working that miracle. I call this the Obama Law.

I say this because people felt as though President Barak Obama had the magic to immediately clean up the huge mess that the previous presidents have made. I am ashamed of the disrespect that the President has to endure. From observation of news clippings and other programs, this Black man is called Obama and not respected as President Obama. Interesting. This section is dedicated to all the teachers operating under the President Obama Law. Keep your head up and continue to strive. Just know that there is at least one individual that sincerely appreciates the work that you do.

One last point in reference to education; I have experienced and observed that there is a large amount of boredom amongst students. The boredom is a result of the curriculum not keeping the attention of the students and the students lacking focus, as many of the Black youth experience at a young age. One day, I had the opportunity of looking at a sixth-grade world history book. I saw where the book touched on the various cultures around the world. There were tributes to great settlers, those that conquered England, and others who did various things around the world. These were the same topics that were taught when I was in school. I am sure that the students, just like me, are uninterested in learning about this history as well.

In one sections of the history book, there was information about Africa. There were pages about tribes and various other topics, but it alarmed me that there was about half a page on Martin Luther King, Jr. (MLK). The book touched on Mahatma Gandhi, which is an interest to Blacks. As I continued to observe, I remember thinking, *so, there are no other great African-Americans that have done anything for this nation?* I totally understand why MLK appears in almost all the history books in America as opposed to Malcolm X or Huey Newton and the Black Panthers Organization. MLK was one of the safest Black leaders to discuss, as far as mass culture in society. He did not come from the standpoint of fighting back or rebellion in the physical sense.

As a result, his methods are more acceptable to mainstream America. Hence, the message to young Blacks is to not fight back, even though brutality is being infringed upon you. Additionally, mainstream Americans believe that Malcolm X and the Panthers were about killing, which is not the case. Think about it, many movements fought for the same thing, freedom, liberty, and liberation; however one method continues to be taught. Why is that? Tricknology and mind control. I say again, please wake up.

Chapter Eleven

College Education

"A loan shark is an entity that loans money at an unbearable interest rate to seek payment at a return. If money is not paid in a timely manner, the loan shark will take by force."
-Charles E. Hill III, M.S.

We are brainwashed into believing that if you are an average tax-paying individual, the way to make it within mainstream society is to obtain an education beyond high school. It is suggested that a college graduate makes more than a high school graduate and a second degree can earn you more than an individual with a bachelor's degree. However, what we are not told or brainwashed to misunderstand is the reality of wage to cost of living, lack of jobs, when trying to pay back the high cost of obtaining the various degrees.

Please understand that education is a great thing. As an adult I continue to try to obtain as much education as possible. Unfortunately, formal education obtained comes with a huge price.

The average family, or better yet the average Black family does not plan for their child/children to attend college from a financial standpoint. It is not that parents do not want to pay for the education of their children, but the reality is that the cost of living makes it hard to accumulate extra savings beyond basic needs. Also parents whom attended college are still paying for their education as well. On average, most Black families are barely making it. We have started to understand that college is now the necessity to obtain a better position in society, within the system. The number of Black college students and Black college graduates has increased. There is an enormous amount of first family graduates, meaning that someone is the first of their family, from generation to generation to graduate.

In my opinion, there are a number of reasons why in 2015 there are still families of first time college graduates. In my family history, my great grandparents where born at the tail end of slavery. My grandmother and siblings were forced into the work field to assist in helping the family. When I say field, I am talking about just that, field work, the same work of slaves. Thus education was not a priority and in fact school was over before it was started. My grandmother had to leave school in the sixth grade to assist in helping the family financially. There was a mode of survival not a mode of education. So in raising her children, what mode is taught, education or the mode in which my grandmother knew? From generation to generation, survival and struggle is what has been passed down.

I am smart enough to understand that life was harder for previous generations, due to Blacks not being able to get a job and the employment obtained were jobs that most of us would not want to do today. I think we have forgotten or have no idea about the hard labor that many Blacks had to endure in order to feed families, or to survive. So when we complain, we need to realize that our ancestors had it far worst. There was no assistance such as unemployment and the jobs were few and far in between. Though things are better for us on the accessibility of jobs, I am not one to take the kibbles and bits and call that eating. Just because things are better does not mean that things are all good.

Blacks as a whole are still struggling, job or no job. As for college, I had a good time meeting new people, experiencing different things; developing as a man, and growing in various other ways. However like most people, I paid for it. College is not in any stretch of the word cheap. In order for me to get ahead in life, to what I was told would position me to create a better life for myself, I had to pay for education. Like all things within the system, college is a huge money maker. It is a business, a big business. Then when you add in sports that are classified as "amateur" athletics, understand the amount of money that schools are getting. College athletes have to be classified as amateurs so that the college students do not get a taste of the massive amounts of money generated from ticket sales, television exposure, merchandise sales, and all other promotion of the athletes.

The point that I am addressing is that college is high in cost and does the end justify the means? When I graduated from college, I thought I would have it made. I was disillusioned to believe that I would be able to get a job that afforded me to pay my bills, buy a car, and live on my own. This was not the case. I obtained my first job working for a corporation making $25,000 a year. As a young college graduate, you have no idea how salary has an impact on you in the beginning as you desire to live as an adult.

I lived with my parents for less than a year, which led to me struggling on my own as I bounced from job to job. Most college graduates know, after six months upon graduating, the government wants back what was loaned to you. In order to make more money and to move towards a better way of living, what do a lot of us do? We enter right back into the system to get another degree, which in turn puts us more in debt.

Allow me to step away for a moment and discuss the good old college payback plan. What do you call a system in place that preys on people that have less and want a chance or opportunity to improve their socioeconomic status? Some may have many names, but I call this person a pimp. Selling your soul by making a deal with the devil is the analogy for it. I am not calling people or situations the devil, but the comparisons are similar. When you make a deal with the devil, there is an agreement to repay at a later date with your soul. Though the payback of student loans are not repayment with your life (though it feels like an eternity to repay), the process in the end feels like you are being pimped.

This is how the process works. You find a school to determine how much money is needed. Once it is determined that you cannot receive the financial aid nor have the trust fund to pay for your education, many of us are faced with tough decisions. The decisions are to work (which the jobs obtained will never pay your tuition from one semester to the next), leave school which we do not want to do, or do what we have to do and that is to get a/or multiple student loans. So once you sign over your life with your name in blood, the meter begins with the cost of the loan and interest accruing. Accruing interest means to begin and add more of a percentage of money to what is owed. It is like pressing a button and money as well as interest is added under your name. Just imagine having your own account where money is placed in the account. As days, months, and years have passed, more money is generated. By the time you graduate, you have at least $30,000 to $40,000 in your account. Well that is being modest because some may have close to $100,000. If the money continues to stay in the account for many years, interest is added which raises the amount to about $50,000 to $60,000. And those with $100,000 the money is raised to $150,000 or even more.

Now who would not want that? Unfortunately the money is your money, but money in reverse; it is the money that you owe. As you are working and trying to make a living for yourself (and family in the future) after graduation, student loans becomes that thorn that you cannot get rid of. Just as the devil reappears to claim what was owed, the government and banks reappear at your door like, "remember me?" Not only do you now owe what you borrowed, you now have to pay the extra money added on by interest and attached fees. Furthermore, one of the terms of the deal is that you are attached to the loan for the life of the loan which is forever. It is similar to serving time in prison and/or a bad marriage.

Most people payback the loans on a thirty plus year basis, a ball and chain for life. With jobs not wanting to pay a salary where one can comfortably afford a house, car, pay bills, and the general cost of living, most struggle to maintain it all. Added to this, is the fact that as long as you have the loan, interest will continue to accrue. As we are attempting to pay off the loans, we continue to get trumped with more money added on to the debt.

In my mind, once I am out of school, I feel as though I should have exceeded the interest that continues to accrue. Such is not the case. I would call this practice loan sharking at its best. "A loan shark is an entity that loans money at an unbearable interest rate to seek payment at a return. If money is not paid in a timely manner, the loan shark will take by force." Just thinking about the struggle to maintain a living makes me think about the theme from the old television show *Good Times* where we are scratching and surviving. Please understand that times have not changed. With the change in the economic structure and job availability, people are barely making it to survive. With trying to have a piece of something, the loss of a job or without an increase in money as the cost of living becomes higher and higher, one cannot pay the loan or in many cases loans.

The government will act as the mob. In a scene from the movie *Goodfellas,* a restaurant owner is not able to make the payments to the mob. The mob's response was, "**** you, pay me." If you cannot make the payments, the government will find a way to get their money back. The government will take your income tax checks and/or garnish your wages. Garnishment of wages is when the government directly takes money out of your paycheck, no matter what. Now if that is not gangsta, then I do not know what is. I ask myself, *Why are we made to do something that America is not doing, pay their debts.* With the forever changing economy, layoffs, high cost of living, capped salaries and wages, I am wondering, was it all worth it?

The interesting thing about college is that it takes on average four to five years to obtain a bachelor's degree. I know that many of you are just like me, graduated with a degree and did not use half of what has been learned in four-five years. I am being modest when I say half. A lot of credits/classes appeared to have been useless in the outside world when it comes to making money and living life. Now, why is that? This reminds me of the song "Everyday Should be the Weekend" by Mass Man, which states "*I remember when I was in school I use to say/ all the stuff they trying to teach be going to waste/ because all this useless information that would go in my brain/ to this day I can't recall or regain/ public schools is a place that train you to be a worker/ instead of being self-sufficient, you dependent and a server."*

Not every enrolled college student had been the top notch high school student. Some students may have attended college summer programs, which are required to assist in development before the school year starts, and I support this concept. However, why do counselors and advisors have you enroll in classes at the beginning of the school year in which credits will not be received? Some students may need the classes, but many do not. My motto is that if you are not ready by the start of the first semester, you are just not ready. The funny thing about the counselors is that they are on the inside and have knowledge and wisdom about what is going on. They do not tell you upfront that the 000 level courses are worthless classes towards graduating. In turn you have wasted time and money; you could have attended a class that would have assisted you in moving forward towards classes to graduate.

The longer you stay in school, "mo' money and mo' money" is provided to the school and system of course. If a school can get you to enroll in additional unnecessary classes, that is more money that the school will obtain. Plus the cost of books for school are ridiculous. Not only are you paying a high cost for school, obtaining worthless amount of information, but now books are hurting your wallet. An edition of a book was good for a course one semester, but then it is no longer acceptable next semester, although it is the same course being taught by the same professor. Why do you think that is? Mo' money, mo' money, which in turn is supply and demand. It is understood that you, the students, need to get the books. No matter how much the book changes, students will purchase the books and not be able to borrow the book from a friend that had the same class.

I do not understand why a business major has to take courses unrelated to business. Why is science a course needed when one has absolutely no interest in science? The classes within your major are basically a two-year structure. Yet four years worth of money is better to receive than two years. With the high cost of tuition, most will have a debt before getting a job or even a degree. Welcome to adulthood.

To break things down a step further, one is at a deficit before he/she begins their life beyond college. It is like the basketball game that started, and you are down in points before the game begins, making it difficult to win. At the end of four years of college, after all the money has been exhausted, either from personal money, grants, scholarships, and loans, most are in debt. Additionally, upon graduating, the institution will request that you "give back" to the school. Now the school wants to bleed me of additional money that I now work for. *Give back?!* So let me get this straight, I now should give back to a school that sucked me dry of money for four to five years. In the words of former Eagles running back Ricky Watters, *"For who, for what?"*

Do not get me wrong, college has cleared the path for many to live a comfortable lifestyle. However, I am willing to bet that there are a larger number of Black college graduates whom do not live that comfortable lifestyle. From the U.S. Census report of 2009[1] (latest information provided in 2012), the average earnings for Caucasians with a bachelor's degree is $57,765, but for Caucasian males it is $71,286. For Blacks, the mean salary is $47,799 and for males it is $55,655. Furthermore if a master's degree is earned, the mean for Caucasians are $73,771 and $91,776 for males compared to $60,067 for Blacks and $68,890 for males. The numbers are lower for women across the board for both cultures as well as other minorities.

The trick was for people to believe that college is the way to afford you the kind of life that you have always dreamed of. With reduced jobs, lack of equated raises/promotions with increased responsibilities, high workloads, jerk bosses, etc., most people do not even like their job. Having a college (bachelor's) degree used to be worth more than it is now. Individuals were worth more in the job market then we are today. Whenever we close the gap, and we being Blacks, the dynamics of that situation tends to change. Examples of this statement are the SAT (Scholastic Aptitude Test), Bachelor's degree, and the Presidential election. When Blacks decreased the gap in scores on the SAT, scoring and components of the test changed. Once we began graduating from college at a higher rate, the bachelor's degree is valued less. A Black president was elected and voting laws are trying to change. Society is now trying to require photo identification in order to vote, after all these years, although there has not been reports of unfairness or cheating at the polls by patrons. Notice that I said cheating by patrons, but yet a law is trying to be passed for photo identification. Thus understand that when we do better, the overall system/structure will change so that our chance of benefits decline.

As I mentioned earlier, before you graduate from school, you are in debt owing the government for wanting to do better as this is what America suggests is the way to become successful. Although in doing so, there is a price tag attached. That price is debt that is stuck to you like a bad marriage. A current college student advises, "If you are going to have to pay for it anyway, pay the least amount possible." Now what exactly does that mean?

A close friend's daughter attended a private college for one and a half years, equivalent to three semesters. Of course the private school was not cheap. To make matters worse, the young lady found out that her completed classes were not credible classes and when she transfers, she had to start over by taking the same or equivalent classes. Subsequently the young lady has to spend more time and yes more money once she transferred to another university. So understand what it is that you are doing and how you are doing it. In finding her way, this young lady has elected to attend the local community college to complete the core classes needed, so that she could transfer to a respected four-year university in the future. Instead of enduring the heavy cost of attending school, she can at least cut the total cost by a quarter or cut it in half.

Think smarter in making decisions about college. Think smarter about the college you attend, the field of work you study, classes taken, and of course the money you do or do not spend. While writing this book, I communicated with a former school mate. He was two grades behind me in high school and went on to receive a Division I AA (Two A) football scholarship to a prestigious private university. As I communicated topics from my book, my friend shared his experiences and one particular story intrigued me.

There was an African-American student, a former football player who performed well academically who spent more than the traditional four or five years in school. It was explained to me that the student was good at everything, so good that it was difficult for him to decide on a profession. He continued to go to school longer than the average four to five years. My friend suggested that the student was well liked by everyone, classified as a "good guy" who stayed out of trouble.

This student campaigned to run for the student body president and had a good chance of winning. To my friend, I stated that he was a young President Barack Obama. My friend replied excitedly, "Yes exactly, just like Barack Obama." Throughout the process there were racist acts and actions he endured. This was during the time when Facebook started to become popular. A rumor started to circulate around the school about either a post or message stating, "No Black man can be president of this university." The wording may not be exact, but you get the point.

In addition to the message on Facebook, the word "Nigger" was spray painted on his door. There were also obscene campus phone calls being made to the student, phone calls full of harassment and racist comments. I was told that the university did not do anything to address these phone calls. When the university was asked to trace the calls, the student was told that they could not be. My friend found out later that the university could indeed trace phone calls, when he was traced for using another student's ID code (calling card) over the phone.

That incident regarding racist actions and various other injustices around that campus sparked reactions within the Black Culture Society, an organization for Blacks. The president of the organization felt as though a change was needed, thus a call for unification among Blacks was implemented. The plan was to raise the awareness for a better curriculum of ethnic value. My friend accurate or not, suggested that there was only one diverse African American studies class. Even if this was not the only African-American studies class, you can see how few the classes were available for African Americans (yet they will take your African American money). He suggested that there were about fifty to seventy members in the organization, but only about four to five people were key factors in making the decisions. The plan by the key members was to plan a walkout, similar to a boycott, by not going to class.

There were other multi-cultural organizations on campus as well, with the thought that maybe these other organizations would link up with the Black Culture Society. That was not the case. As the group planned and organized, the president felt as though they needed to keep the strategy to themselves. The reason for this way of thinking was that just because all the members were Black did not mean that all were in support of the cause and that there would be some Blacks that would sellout by telling.

Things were quiet all the way up until the day that the plan was supposed to be executed. Right before the walkout was going to occur there was a general sense that something was wrong. As the team relied on the unity and support of the people, the people had other agendas. When I say people, I am speaking about the Black students. Things were brought to a halt because there was no power in the movement. There is strength in numbers, yet in this case the numbers had dwindled smaller and smaller. The movement and plan were lost.

Now one may ask why this story was important enough to share. First I think that the story was interesting. I also wanted to illustrate how colleges do not have good intentions with us in mind, though they take our money. Not all situations and universities are not like this. There are many universities that welcome individuals that come from various communities and walks of life. Now that I am older and wiser, I wonder when did Black colleges lose its value for Blacks to attend. I say this as if I attended a Black college myself, which I did not.

My path and life did not extend to a Black college after high school. The high school guidance counselor did not have a great view about historically Black universities and colleges (HBCU).

Without passing judgment, but I could not expect a Caucasian man, from the country to understand or guide young Blacks to a HBCU As a result of the brainwashing that went on at my school, there weren't particularly too many Blacks that enrolled in non-traditional colleges. As an adult now, I believe my mindset is give back to Black. If I am going to extend my education and give money, why not give it to a university to support the entity that will assist people just like me? Wh would I not give people just like me an opportunity to change their lives? On the other hand, there are some HBCUs that I would not have attended. If there is a strong HBCU that could have given me what I needed, I would definitely have attended if I could have done it all over again.

As I currently understand the history of why HBCUs were started, it makes me have a great appreciation for the overall goal that was in mind. One should not forget where life started. Without HBCUs, Blacks would not have been college educated. So now that things have changed within the world around us, we no longer support the system that was there for us. Though we are not fully accepted at various, prestigious, well-known mainstream universities, we tend to give our money to schools that in a large part really did not want us there.

On a side note, I would love for greatness to be restored back to HBCUs. College athletics is a big financial business. Schools get millions of dollars for television contracts, bowl games, and making the NCAA tournament. I would love to see top notch dollars be contributed to HBCUS, which can help us move forward. I anticipate the day when Howard University or some other HBCU has a Fab Five, make it to the Final Four NCAA basketball tournament, and even win the championship. I did not attend a HBCU and would not contribute money back to the university that I attended. I would give back to a HBCU, giving back to Black which is what we as Blacks are suppose too. And if not us that gives back to Black, then who will?

Chapter Twelve

College Basketball- Black Exploitation

"While college athletics have unceasingly benefited whites, these same institutions have unduly failed black student-athletes."[1]

College basketball is an important topic to discuss, due to the exploitation of Black male athletes. Collegiate athletics is a system that is deemed as amateur competition. As stated previously, it has to be classified as such in order for the millions of dollars consumed by the events are not divided amongst the players. If the likes of Kevin Garnett, Kobe Bryant, Dwight Howard, LeBron James, and all other basketball players who have successfully jumped from high school to the National Basketball Association (NBA), why is it important for all other players to attend college for one year?

It is clear that the financial gains and marketing of the college players are far greater than allowing the athletes to jump to the pros. It is said that players should attend college to mature and for further development of their basketball skills.

To go against reasons stated for the induction of the one year in college, veterans who have developed the maturity in college have also engaged in acts that are deemed as lacking in maturity by way of their actions and decisions made off of the basketball court. So, is the rule about age or about the individual themselves? Not all young players have transitional problems and not all older players avoid problems. There are players that compete for four years of college only to get cut after a few seasons in the NBA. In fact, some of the top players at the collegiate level that turned out to become busts in the NBA, can also be guys that spent four years in college. So there should not be a question about the development of a player's talent and skills. In America, college students are regulated to attend college, but foreign players in other countries are young professionals being paid for their talents. If good enough, these foreign players are drafted to play for the NBA. So again, is that one year in college really necessary?

The arguments appeared justified for the reasons why basketball players have to compete for one year in college. In my opinion, I feel as though the arguments are rather weak.

In what other sports, besides football, are there stipulations to where players cannot compete as a professional? There are no stipulations in golf, tennis, hockey, boxing, or baseball. College basketball, with the National Collegiate Athletic Association (NCAA) tournament, ticket sales, advertising, marketing, television deals, and merchandising, produces huge profits and benefits. It is better to exploit players for the unnecessary yet forced one year of college as opposed to no years of exploitation. It is clear that the financial gain by marketing players is far greater than allowing the athletes to jump to become professionals.

There are individuals that I am sure were upset that they could not earn money off of the likes of Kobe Bryant, Kevin Garnett, Amare Stoudemire, and LeBron James by way of collegiate basketball. Can you imagine the exploitation of LeBron James at the collegiate level?

It is obvious that basketball is a predominantly Black sport. During the era of segregation, Blacks could not compete at the schools that now fight so hard to sign elite high school Black players. Such universities as North Carolina, Duke, Kentucky, and Michigan, and many others were not accepting of the Black athletes. The only schools Blacks could attend were Black colleges and universities. All of the top Black players attended predominately Black schools, which benefited the schools.

When it was understood that Blacks could bring in millions of dollars and revolutionize the college game, changes were made, thus the exploitation of the Black athlete. Again, we were only good enough because of the lure of money.

The Fab Five – (Exploited)

The Fab Five consisted of five of the top freshmen college basketball players in the nation, who attended Michigan University. Like so many, we watched as they revolutionized the game and culture of college basketball. These five inner-city freshmen played at the same time, trash talking and playing with a certain kind of confidence and swag that had never been seen before at the collegiate level. They sported bald heads and wore long shorts, black sneakers, and socks.

For two years they delighted many and inflamed others. Those that come from similar backgrounds can identify with the game exhibited by the Fab Five. Conversely, those that come from a more mainstream environment tend to have rejected the style and play of the young urban, cocky kids that played basketball.

It is not determined that the Fab Five exhibited that same cockiness off the court, but they were judged by many as such. They exemplified an "I don't care" attitude on the basketball court that did not necessarily define who they were as individuals.

However, because of the public forum, it was easy to take verbal shots at the young Black men.

From watching the documentary, *The Fab Five*, it was shocking to learn of the blatant disrespect that occurred back in the 1990's. The high level of disrespect came from the alumni of the university they attended. The disrespect involved not only people being critical of how they played the game, but race was also in question. The players were called "niggers" and other names that are deemed prejudice. They (the alumni) sent the school letters that basically said that they (the alumni) do not want Blacks from the hood to represent the almighty MU. To me that showed the ignorance of what some Michigan graduates represented at that time. Those that graduated from Michigan, those that sent in letters, tried to give the impression as if they are righteous individuals. This is similar to incidents that occurred during marches in the 1950's and 60's.

When Blacks nonviolently marched to protest equality, ignorance, and hatred were displayed. First it was the crowd throwing things, which incited violence. The law played a part as well in allowing incidents to occur. We were watered down as if we were on fire in a blaze. Dogs were released on us but for what reason? The hatred that was being expressed from the alumni of

MU was not righteous nor was there, (no depiction from the documentary) any action taken by the university to protect its players from hate relations from alumni.

In the case of the alumni at Michigan, they felt as though they were righteous in their decisions. Why should the players have had to endure that type of treatment and from fellow alumni at that? Again the criticism was not just about basketball, but about race also.

Though these players were celebrities, stars in their own right, they could not escape being pimped. The Fab Five put fans in the stands, which allowed the university to make huge amounts of money. Of course none of the players received any of the proceeds. This would be equivalent to Denzel Washington selling out at the box office and not receiving any of the profits. Many young professional entertainers receive money for services, yet a professional college basketball player cannot because they are in college?

There are numerous trained professional basketball players that came straight out of high school that did not need the one year of college. All that one year does is take possible money away from the players and their families. The money provides the universities, head of merchandising companies, and others that are involved with the profit of gains and returns.

I like to call this good old legal pimpin'. Michigan exploited the talents of the five freshmen to receive and gain huge profits. Though money was made, the treatment in which the Fab Five received was nothing but tricknology. It was alleged that Chris Webber had taken money from a booster of some sort. As a result, the team's accomplishments have been erased from history of Michigan athletes. From the documentary, it also suggests that the players cannot step foot onto campus for a duration of years. If that is not a slap in the face, I do not know what is. It looks like a matter of taking the money and running.

It was documented that in the two years which the Fab Five played, the school reported a ten million dollar gain. The players' merchandise was sold just as LeBron James or Kobe Bryant's merchandise sells in the professional arena. Consequently, money was being made without a clear consent or authorization of the players.

At the collegiate level, before one can participate in sports from high school, there is a document called the NCCA Clearing House. It is the registration of rules and guidelines used in order to participate in college athletics. Not getting into all the particulars of this agreement, there is an underlying clause within the documentation. Do understand how this trick works. As a high school athlete being recruited by various schools, one desires to compete at the next level. In order to do so, one has to be cleared by the Clearing House. I can recall when I was in school that teammates were delayed from competition because they did not sign this agreement. Understand that it is mandatory, and one will sign this document so that they can compete. The document is signing over your professional rights as an athlete, so the only financial benefit you receive is the yearly scholarship. The money being made from your efforts of competition is being consumed by all others because you are deemed an "amateur" competitor and not a professional. Again I call that good pimpin'.

Chapter Thirteen

<u>Welfare</u>

"We spend billions of dollars on welfare, yet millions are trapped on welfare. It's not worth their while going to work."[1]
-David Cameron

The one thing I learned from my high school economics class is that nothing in life is free. My teacher told me that if something is free, somebody is paying for it. The welfare system within the Black community provides services that many families know all too well. I am not suggesting that other cultures do not conspire to receive government assistance themselves, but again I tend to focus on what it is that we are doing.

The definition of welfare is a statutory procedure or social effort designed to promote the basic physical and material well-being of people in need.[2] Welfare is also classified as the financial or other aid provided, especially by the government to the people in need.[3] An additional definition is receiving regular assistance from the government or private agencies because of need.

I recall being embarrassed as a kid because my family was a part of the welfare system. Although welfare assisted us as we needed it, it was still an embarrassment in regards to pride. When my mom wanted me to go to the store, I was ashamed to do so with the fake money. What mortified me even more was that if I had to go to the store with ten dollars or more in food stamps, I had to carry the booklet to verify that I was the holder of the food stamps.

When my friends asked to go to the store with me, I would suggest that they stay on the block until I got back. However, they insisted on tagging along. Eventually the cat was out of the bag. Yes we were poor! The same friends from the same poor neighborhood that acted like their families were not on food stamps were too in the system as well. I observed that they sometimes carried that same booklet as I did. Though we lived within a poor community, we did not feel that we were poor until we had to carry the food stamps. Some of my friends tried to justify that they were only carrying the booklet by way of the good old barter system. For those who do not know about the barter system, it is an exchange of goods and services. To make it simple, five dollars of real money gets you ten dollars of food stamps.

In case there is still denial, the reality is that if you are on welfare or assistance, you are poor or better yet underneath the line of poverty. If individuals were adequate, then assistance would not be needed. Now do not get me wrong, due to current poor economic conditions, assistance is needed even for the everyday working class. However, assistance should be designed for just that, to assist. Assistance is defined as the provision of money, resources, or information to help someone.[4] Assistance should not be used to excel one in life to where he/she can maintain a lifestyle without working. Assistance should not be the way of life or the addiction that keeps you coming back. Welfare should be the help needed to carry you and your family to the next level so that welfare is no longer needed. I know many families that have been a part of the welfare system all of their lives and have no plans to achieve better then where they are.

The concern that I have is that parents use welfare as a way of life. Welfare will be the only means of income that some parents will ever work for. The sad part about it is that the same lessons are past down to the next generations. Society has come to understand that the higher number of children conceived results in more obtainable money and benefits. As a result, children are produced not out of love, but for survival or a check. Think about that for a moment. A whole life is created for payment and not for the love of life. Added to this is the fact that the parent(s) cannot even afford the kids. If one can afford additional children, the assistance would not be needed.

In many cases within a Black structure, the mother and father have no plans of being together. As in many Black families, the man is not present. Therefore, in many cases, the women raise the children herself.

My sister made a powerful statement to me once, though I do not know if she herself coined the phrase. She said, "There are a lot of men operating as men from a woman's perspective." I found this to be compelling in interpretation. The statement suggests that there are many homes in which boys are guided and directed by women. Also as I observed the behaviors and actions of men, I now know why some men act as they do. Though I am a Black man as well, I am unbiased and co-sign the fact that there is sadness when it comes to the limited representation of the strong Black man in society. I say that due to the countless families that are destroyed at the hands of men. Fatherless children that do not get a chance to receive the security from their fathers or the guidance a child needs in life.

"Any fool with a _____ can make a baby, but only a real man can

raise his children." -Furious Styles, *Boyz in the Hood.*[5]

So do understand that a father provides and is involved with their children. There are many that act as a donor whom provided one half of the ingredients to a woman and is either not around, or inconsistent in raising their children. In observation, there are a lot of donors in the world.

This is not a plot to condemn the Black man. As men we have to think about our actions and how we affect others. I mean if you are a single man doing what you do, it is what it is by way of engaging in sexual encounters with women. Yet when you bring children into the mix or take the steps in being a responsible parent, I think that is the time to grow up and assume take care of your responsibilities as a man. This holds true for women as well. Once children are entered into the equation, one's life should change with responsible actions for the children. All in all, it is about the children. So in the case that a man is not providing or what is being provided is not enough, welfare becomes the option for many to raise children, live, and survive.

One thing that I want to clarify is that I am not here to man bash or downgrade the Black man. If we keep it real, there is a huge disparity in what I am speaking about. If not, if I am wrong for what I am saying, I would love for anyone to educate me on what I observe, discuss, and work with on an everyday basis. Trust, if I am for the betterment of Black people, why would I not want to discuss the overall greatness of Black men? If I am going to talk about our problems, then I am going to talk about them. So instead of thinking that I am dogging Black men, take this as a plea for us to be better men, as well as better fathers to where our children are guided by us as men.

I would like to encourage young people, is if you cannot take care of yourself, why would you bring a child into this world that you cannot afford? Not only do some people have one child, but they will have multiple children that they cannot afford. Now tell me what sense does that make?

I consider myself to have received the basic education in school, so I understand that zero minus three equals negative three (03= -3). I say this because zero dollars plus three kids equals negative three additional individuals to provide for. Not only is it a negative in the monetary sense, but it is also a negative in what is needed for the overall development for the children. If the mother and father are not together in raising the children, that is the first negative for the children before discussing money issues, problems, and other concerns. So there is no need to go further with that point. When there is a lack of money and resources to raise a family, welfare becomes the savior of the family. The money received from welfare is a poverty stricken lifestyle. The money provided is not money that a working citizen can live and feed his/her family. I see this kind of struggle often in my close relation to our people.

I am not passing judgment on families that are a part of the welfare system. Some may say that I am doing so in my discussion on what people do and how they do it. Speaking about various observed situations of people or how things are wrong is not judgment, in my opinion. The things that people do are all open for discussion depending on what is being done. For example, I had a conversation with a woman that talked about her friend and how she parents. The friend of the lady that I know left her sleeping three-year-old in the house at night so she could go across the street to drink and party with neighbors. As we talked about it, the woman that I knew said that we needed to end the conversation because we were judging her friend. I suggested that the conversation was not about judgment, but about speaking about a wrong of a child.

Again a lot of my opinions are not for judgment but to get us to think about things differently. So if anyone feels as though I am judging families for being on public assistance, I apologize for the misconception.

To have more children for more money is a detriment within itself. Detriment is defined as the state of being harmed or damaged or a cause of harm or damage.[6] Having additional children when there is no money, lack of hope, and poverty is in more cases then not, a detriment to society. There has to be some form of boundaries created to where welfare should not be the way of life. I could go on to list other things that cause harm to children by way of lack, such as resources, money, time, but I will not. What I have mentioned in this section is enough for things to be rough for a child in development as he or she gets older.

What I am trying to say is that we need to think more about our choices and decisions we make. We need to not think about welfare as a benefit in which to raise our children. If people will be honest and understand some aspects about dating, in most cases when a man spends money on a woman, please know that the money is not "free." There is some form of compensation that the man is going to want in return at some point. If that is the case in dating, why would one fail to think that the "free" money that the state/government provides does not come with some form of control attached, a hidden agenda, or something wanted in return?

For those that do not know, control is attached to welfare, which I will break down from my point of view. Without getting into specific numbers or details, the amount of money given is a form of control. A household that utilizes welfare services cannot have a man within the same house, so I cannot say family that is on welfare. A single parent (mother) is controlled by how much money she can make if she did go out to get a job. If the parent is capable of making more money than provided, welfare would not be needed. As the dollar amount working does nothing to excel the household income, it would be better to stay within that control of welfare.

Another form of control is where a household can live. About a year ago, I watched *The Isaiah Thomas Story* that aired on public television. Isaiah Thomas is a popular former basketball player that won two championships with the Detroit (Bad Boy) Pistons. As the story portrayed his life, I took notice to a situation that occurred by way of welfare and reforms made within the system. Isaiah's mother, a welfare recipient received a letter suggesting that because she was on welfare, she and her family had to move from their current residence to the projects. As the story proceeded, the mother's friend received the same letter, bit the bait and moved to the projects. Isaiah's mother fought for her family by pleading her case to local politicians and by pleading her case, she did not have to move. Unfortunately the mother's friend who had moved was severely beate and injured while living in the projects. The point of that story illustrated the bad foreseen conditions of the environment within the project community which welfare assisted to create.

There was also a documentary I watched on Netflix that discussed circumstances on the same lines. The documentary was called *The Pruitt-Igoe Myth*, a very compelling depiction of what happened to form the first projects in St. Louis. In other words, this was population control.

A project can be defined as a collaborative enterprise, frequently involving research or design that is carefully planned to achieve a particular aim. Projects can be further defined as temporary rather than permanent social systems that are constituted by teams within or across organizations to accomplish tasks under time constraints.

So what was the aim of the projects? I would classify a project as an experiment, but an experiment at whose cost?

The *Urban Dictionary* has a definition that sparks additional elaboration. It says "public housing" or "project homes" is a form of housing tenure in which the property is owned by a government authority, which may be central or local.[7]

A quick note, I encourage everyone to please look at the documentaries that I speak of to observe parallels in one's life or for more understanding of what is really going on. The thing that impacted me the most was the process of moving Blacks and other poor people into a controlled environment. I grouped Blacks and poor people together because both are equal in how we are judged and both fight for the same cause. Poor people alike face the same conditions universally and are all looked at as less than in the overview of society, no matter what culture.

In watching the documentary, I observed a great deal of information. The project buildings were newly renovated and yes suitable living conditions when built so one can see where the attraction and persuasion would come in where individuals wanted to live. The buildings were public housing, represented by the public housing authority. Everything in my eyes that is "public" for Blacks are always not quite efficient. For instance, public schools (lacks educating and is less equipped than other schools), public assistance (assistance but yet poverty), public defendant (lawyers that bargain for plea deals), and public housing (projects or other housing areas usually unsafe socially and economically poor). Thus, "public" in my opinion is less than and less efficient.

Getting back to the documentary, I watched as once again those on welfare were told to move into the projects due to the benefits being received. Additionally there were stipulations of control attached with the move. A woman shared that in order for her to receive welfare benefits, the man (Black man) could not be present within the family structure. Do people understand why I discuss the absence of the fathers in the home and how huge it is? It is bigger than what many of us may think. Going backwards to move forward is what is needed sometimes. Looking back in what was used to break us down, slavery and how the removal of the men/fathers from the homes kills the total foundation as a whole in which a strong man within the home provided a stronger family unit. The slave masters were taught to divide the family by taking the male slave out of the family so that there is more of an inferiority of the family, thus not having to be concerned about togetherness or rebellion. Yet again welfare is a division of the family unit.

Another stipulation in *The Pruitt-Igoe Myth* was once moved into the projects, families could not own a television. To enforce this rule, the projects were monitored periodically by social workers through random visits. I found it interesting that the elected officials found a way to get money to fund the buildings, but could not find any money for the maintenance of the buildings once occupied by the people.

As the buildings were new, the buildings were taken care of and well kept. Over time there was no maintenance or upkeep of the buildings, just as most things occupied Black and public. This had to have been an organized effort/idea due to similar occurrences that happened in other areas within the United States. For example, it is understood that Philadelphia, New York City, Chicago, Boston, and just about every big city have had the same project housing experience in one form or another. Why is that? Various individuals made a lot of money from the experiment and others were told how to make a profit off the poor/Blacks. Communication of profit are the same as contract leasing and other means of making money in which Blacks or poor people pay the price.

As it stated in the documentary in a matter of words, housing poor people is big business. Due to the massive amount of money made, projects appear or appeared in various cities around the United States. In most areas, the word "projects" (in the housing concept) usually has a negative stigma attached to it. I knew some men and women that would not date someone that lived in the projects, which is considered to be an area that possesses many issues and socioeconomic problems.

With what was said within the documentary and my interpretation, it is clear that population control and money is what the experiment was about. A certain group or class of people placed in an environment under the worst conditions, resources, education, and fewer opportunities offered are expected to achieve as if the playing field is equally leveled. One must climb that mountain without knowledge or support and be expected to be good enough. Yes I agree that some do make it, but the sum of achievement is not close to those that do not.

The main issue here is welfare a benefit or not? As some see it as a benefit, lifestyle, or survival, I call it a trap for many. It is a way of support or survival that can be cut at any time. Already the benefits are starting to be cut from the system. To me this is similar to slaves being freed into what? To cut families, excuse me, to cut women and children off of welfare means what?

As some view assistance and control as a benefit, please do understand what the tricknology behind that assistance and what price is paid when benefits are cut. I am hoping that by writing this, I touch people to where they rethink the plan for assistance and having children that they can afford so welfare is not an option. Focus more on thinking and better planning instead of poverty or being trapped. If assistance is needed, use it for just that, assistance. That means using benefits for a specific amount of time while creating plans to obtain a position where assistance is no longer needed. Either way you look at it, one will have to make a move off of welfare, whether you are kicked off or the children become older to where benefits are no longer received. So when that happens, then what?

Chapter Fourteen
Jail/Prison

"Large areas or populated residents of Blacks across the United States from generation to generation."

-Charles E. Hill III, M

A prison is a place in which people are physically confined and deprived of personal freedom. Freedom is being free from being owned by other people, companies, corporations or government. Freedom is the opposite of slavery. Prison is just that, the lack of freedom and being owned by people, companies, corporations, or a government. When prison and/or human ownership is spoken of, what is being stated? I like to say, "The Black man is a target." Again when I say Black man, I am also speaking of the Black woman as well as the target of imprisonment. Where did it start? Prison basically started when Africans were shipped over from Africa. We were (and still are) cheap labor to make someone else rich or their lives better by cheap labor that fuel huge profit.

As stated previously, slavery is a form of prison, which was illustrated using comparisons in an earlier chapter. What needs to be recognized and understood is the clear deception and tricknology that many cannot see. A great trick is when the magician is able to elude the people. The illusion is a trick, a con, and/or deception. A magic trick is no different than the various beliefs that there were open arms regarding equality. There was no equality then and there is no equality now.

An example of this is the drastic academic gap, the prison population, the unemployment rate in America, and the many negative statistics in society in which Blacks/African Americans are at the top. This is a position that continues to be held year after year and generation after generation. One cannot believe that all issues and negatives for Blacks stem from a culture standpoint and that Blacks want to be associated with the negativity within society. There are many factors and odds that are against Blacks that contribute to some of the widespread gaps that are negative for us. In the Black community, there are people that believe that fairness and equality exist. Yet the majority of Blacks know that things have never been fair, even with the law and law enforcement. This point is evident in the rate of incarceration among Blacks compared to other cultures and the justice experienced and observed in present day Black America. Unfair verdicts given to Blacks or cases that did not provide justice for Blacks contribute to the large gap.

For example, the Emmitt Till case resulted in a not guilty verdict, although evidence was provided and witnesses testified about what occurred. Rodney King was beaten on tape and there was no conviction for those who committed the crime. Some may argue that these cases were decades ago so there are more current examples.

During the process of writing I watched the Allen Iverson story, "No Crossover." It was interesting to me how the judge was able to sentence a young Black teen to an excessive amount of time in prison. Allen Iverson was ordered to serve fifteen years in prison for a bowling alley brawl, yet we had to fight for an investigation of George Zimmerman in the murder of Trayvon Martin. Notice that I did not say the conviction of George Zimmerman, but an investigation. And as we all witnessed, he was deemed not guilty of murder.

Here you can see how unity has helped in making changes due to the outcomes of these two situations. The unified pressure applied to the justice system helped in the release of Allen Iverson. Pressure applied towards the Sanford police department led to George Zimmerman being charged with second degree murder though the outcome was not what Blacks felt was right or just. Unity and pressure in the Jenna 6 case helped the young men receive freedom for what should have not, in my opinion at least merited a conviction. Please do not overlook how unity and coming together works in our favor. And for those that do not know or have never heard of the Jenna 6 case, I encourage one to research Google, Wikipedia, or YouTube for a better understanding.

What plays in my mind is the massive amount of time in jail that Allen Iverson had been given for the type of crime he committed. Though Iverson had a celebrity status during his brush with the law, he was incarcerated. I mean, we would have never known "The Answer" and the other aspects we were privileged to see in regards to Iverson, well at least here in Philadelphia. I am not saying that crimes are acceptable. A bowling alley brawl is not worthy of a fifteen-year sentence. And the fact that a judge can get away with doing so is something within itself.

In Michael Moore's movie, *Capitalism: A Love Story*[1], various corporate crimes are detailed in regards to robbery of the American people. There still have not been any convictions to the crimes committed. Why is that? In *Training Day*[2], Denzel Washington shared with Ethan Hawk, "That's a high roller dog."

Denzel illustrated that if an individual who has high-level status, he/she would be untouchable. I guess such is the case with the corporations in Moore's movie.

If I can go back to my point for a minute, Iverson had a celebrity status, what about those who are not celebrities and are given unfair sentences? Do understand that Allen Iverson was seen to have had great potential as an athlete; there was a fight for him to become free. There are untold cases where the charges do not equal the crime. In 1935, W.E.B. Du Bois shared, "African Americans were criminalized for committing Black Code-type crimes and often were subject to tougher sentences than those imposed upon whites convicted of similar crimes."

The definition of Black Code is a popular name given to statutes passed by pro-slavery, southern states of the USA before and after the Civil War in order to limit the civil rights of slaves or freed slaves, which was an attempt to assert some kind of continued prejudice against blacks.[3] All Black Codes were eventually repealed. These same attitude and behaviors still apply currently.

In present day society I feel as though Black Codes still exist. Although I do not condone the sale of drugs, I do not desire to see

Black men rotting in prison when other cultures are not punished for the same exact crime. I have always thought the law that gives more prison time to individuals who were caught with crack cocaine as opposed to those who get caught with larger amounts of cocaine was always unfair.

"Despite recent federal reforms of crack sentencing laws, much higher penalties exist for possession and sale of crack, despite the fact that pharmacologically it is the same drug as cocaine. Simple possession of 28 grams of crack cocaine yields a five-year mandatory minimum sentence for a first offense; it takes 500 grams of powder cocaine to prompt the same sentence."[4]

Now allow me to say this, I do not approve of the use or selling of crack/cocaine. This epidemic has destroyed an enormous amount of young Black lives, Black communities, and Black families. There is nothing positive from the sell or use of the white substance, as it is being distributed or consumed within the communities. Crack in the Black community can be viewed as a form of genocide.

The original point that I wanted to make behind the time given to those who are caught with crack versus cocaine is that crack is the cheaper drug. If you think about it, who consumes or possesses crack cocaine? Who possesses more of the purer high cost substance? So when a Black individual is caught with the small amount of crack "cocaine", he/she was given a longer jail sentence than the individual that is caught with the larger amount of cocaine. Less time is given for the purer form of cocaine, even though they both are cocaine. These acts of conviction are lawfully justified.

Crack is the drug for the poor and those with less money. Pure cocaine protected the rich from receiving the large amount of time that Blacks and others have received, another form of tricknology. It does not stop there. The trick is making people believe that there was a strong push to change the law (crack versus cocaine), because the imbalance was unfair. Due to the fact that the law convicted large amounts of Blacks, the imbalance was not fair to Blacks. It has never been fair since the inception of the law. However, the law had taken on a different meaning when more Caucasians began to indulge in the cheaper form of cocaine.

The laws have been changed. Now the epidemic is no longer just a Black thing. In my opinion, drugs should have never have been classified as a "Black" thing. We did not have the money or other means to bring drugs into the country. Blacks and poor people only saw a way to earn income due to the lack of opportunities. A person having the opportunity to make ten thousand dollars or more would look attractive to a person who is starving and does not see an opportunity to even make five hundred dollars within the American system due to not fitting within the workforce in America. If we are realistic, working minimum wage or any job that pays low is just not going to cut it within this economy.

In this stage of my life, I do not think that I could work hard at McDonald's only to receive an inadequate amount of money at the end of the pay period. No I am not saying that I am better than the individuals whom work in that capacity. I will say that I have taken advantage of opportunities presented to me where I am able to maintain a lifestyle where criminal activity does not cross my mind due to lack of opportunities.

One would never say that they would not aspire to take drastic measure outside of the law if opportunities within the current American system did not seem obtainable. The thought that comes to mind is a person that sells drugs is condemned for what he/she has done. Desperate times call for drastic measures. That individual may be starving and sees drug dealing as the only mean of eating. I believe that people need to understand that there are some people that do not fall within the ideal American society. These individuals will never be productive laborers within the community. Therefore they take opportunities when they are given. And these opportunities may not be within the confines of the law, thus negative and immoral, but yet an opportunity for some.

Once the street corner dealer is placed in jail, there will be someone else that will take over, which continues the cycle. If you want to solve a problem, getting to the root is the answer. Jail, drugs, and the continuation of crime is a way for the prison system to keep going. More jails are being built to harbor individuals for large sums of money. By not getting an education or at least creating options for yourself is nothing outside of the plan and trap for you. Please believe that there will be plenty of prisons and detention centers to warehouse all unwanted guests, those that do not cease opportunity and understand the American way of living.

Chapter Fifteen
<u>Private</u> <u>Prison</u>

"Jail is another place where all the violence is/ poverty in the streets come from policies of our politics.
-Mass Man, "Somewhere in the World"

A private or for-profit prison, jail, or detention center is a place in which individuals are physically confined or interned by a third party, which is contracted by a government agency.[1] Private prison companies typically enter into contractual agreements with government that commit prisoners and then pay a per diem or monthly rate for each prisoner confined in the facility. The prison system has become a way to inherit wealth for major companies and corporations.

Formulated in 1984, the Corrections Corporation of America (CCA) is given private government contracts to overtake prisons in order to facilitate profit. This means the CCA acts as planners to create the business plan and operations, which ensures the production of money. What makes the money? Money is in crime, lack of education, lack of opportunities, ignorance (ig-no-rance of what's going on), greed, and lack of rehabilitation. Chris Rock once said, "The money is not in the core, but in the comeback."

Wikipedia states "the recidivism rate for prisoners released from prison within one year is 44.1%; this number rises to 67.5%

within three years of being released from prison."[2] Prisoners whom have received an education in prison are most likely to not return. "Prison education has been shown to successfully reduce the recidivism rate for released prisoners which one could say education sparks rehabilitation. In the US, the rate of recidivism within three years of release is found to be between 43.3% and 51.8%."[2] Those prisoners released, who received an education, had a significantly lower rate of recidivism. People should understand that education is the light that shines bright with hope and opportunity in moving forward in life.

If education is the way, why is money being put into the prison system and less in the education system? Well at least this appears to be the case within the inner cities across the United States of America. If one can think and observe, one can decipher the plot of what is happening. In the state of Pennsylvania, Governor Tom Corbett made some interesting budget cuts that fall right in line with what is discussed in this chapter. Since I am a rebellious non-news watching, non-paper reading individual, news seems to present itself to me as needed. I was told how Tom Corbett proposed to cut funding for public education spending by $1.1 billion dollars. From various websites and other forms of mass media, I learned about how Corbett reduced funding in higher education (college/universities) as well as grant money, mental health services, and public assistance.

Think about how many jobs were lost and how many more people now live further under the level of poverty. So with the money reduced in education, one would think that the problem is money. If money is an issue or a concern, how can money be used to fund additional prisons or for the expansion of prisons? If there is no money, there is no money. Right? Doesn't this also send a message about what is valued more in our society? Money is taken from education and increased for prison rehabilitation.

What exactly is rehabilitation? Rehabilitation is defined as to restore to good health or useful life, as through therapy and education; to reinstate the good name of, and to restore the former rank, privileges, or rights of.[3] Now maybe I really do not know personally the concept of rehabilitation, but from the outside looking in, rehabilitation is failing. As the definition stated, rehabilitation is achieved through education and therapy. Again education has been reduced or cut all together. Rehabilitation is to reinstate the good name of. If we will keep it real for a moment and admit that once an individual return from prison, his/her name is not restored back to good. If that was the case, individuals would be able to obtain employment to where

re-offending is not the means for survival. With the retention rate

of prisoners reoffending, I ask, is prison a system of rehabilitation

or a for-profit industry?

I recall watching a program on the Public Broadcasting

Service (PBS) network. The title of the program eludes me;

however the program discussed private prisons in a town

called Harding, located in Montana. According to PBS, the town

suffered so much economically that the town is becoming

extinct, similar to a ghost town. In order to save the town, the

idea was to resurrect the town by generating money through

the building of a prison. The CCA, the nation's leading provider

of correctional solutions to federal, state, and local

government, was contacted to develop the plan to

"rehabilitate" (in other words, to make money).

Prisons and prisoners have always been a source of big

money for the American system and for those that run the

prisons. As I shared earlier, prison and slavery go hand and

hand. Slavery has been abolished as illegal, where the other is

legal. As a result of reduced opportunities or a lack of

understanding of the system, people resort to circumstances

that they deem necessary at the time to survive. I am not saying in all cases, but in many cases, crimes have become the way of survival for some individuals. Some people live a life without understanding how to function in society and to avoid performing criminal activities. By the time some people acknowledge the current direction of their lives, which is a spiral of prison life, it is too late.

"This is for my niggas that's too broke to pay attention/ here's a little freestyle I just hope that they will listen/ you see they mind is on their money, but it's fogging up they vision/ and bout time they open they eyes it's too late, cuz they wake up in prison."

-Mass Man, "How I Feel"

I am not an advocate of crime, but I am not for reduced education and lack of opportunities, which leaves people lost and wondering how to be successful within a society that only has one concern: money. Once an individual comes out of prison with no education and a charge to his/her name, how is survival accomplished without resorting back to the life that resulted in prison? This is no different than when slaves were set free from the plantation into a world that they did not have the skills in order to adapt and thrive.

In no way am I suggesting that upon being released from prison that making it and finding your way is impossible. Re-offending is most likely the plan because individuals have no other means to survive. With the three-strikes-and-you-are-out rule, these individuals will most likely be confirmed to jail for life. If you have never played the game of baseball and the pitcher has played all of his or her life, it would be easy for you to strike out. Plus, if the baseball bat you use is smaller, the game is over before it even started. Can you see where I am going here?

The reason why I am writing this is to not only shed light to those in darkness but to also offer guidance to young people and individuals in hopes of assisting them in understanding the process of tricknology. By learning the tricks of the trade early on, they may be able to avoid getting caught up in the systematic web that could be impossible to get out of.

It is understood that reduced education is when there are reduced opportunities later in life, where money is made off of the desperation of people trying to survive. People have to understand that money will be made just as money had been made off of Blacks even when slavery ended. As discussed earlier, when slavery ended or slaves were not forced to reside on the plantation, production of work did not end. Contract or convict leasing was formed, which meant that Blacks were contracted out from the prison system. Blacks were thrown in prison on charges that would stick, even if they were innocent. So understand that Blacks were picked up and thrown in prison in order to complete work. With the expansion of various prisons, this means "mo' money, mo' money, mo' money." Like always, Blacks (not solely Blacks, but other poor people) will be at the root of that money being made for the benefit of others. Time, lack of opportunities, enough disparity, lack of concern, or lack of thinking is all that is needed before a crime is committed and individuals will fall right in line with the master plan, or better yet, the Master's plan.

As I am writing, I came across an article/website entitled "Corrections, Private Prisonization"[4], which discussed a wealth of powerful information. I read that in 1970, there were two hundred eighty thousand prisoners compared to two billion prisoners in 2000 in the United States. Of course more prisons plus more prisoners equals more money.

The fact is that investors, who were friends with legislatures, adopted the CCA and other organizations where able to setup expansion of prisons. The article and website discussing the CCA shared how, "correctional Corporations have amassed large political influences through government ties, lobbying power and campaign contributions, while attempting to convert the discourse or justice into the language of the marketplace, claiming to run prisons more efficiently and cheaper, doing a better job and saving taxpayers money."[4] In my opinion, and I may stand alone in this, most individuals that are out for profit are not thinking about the needs of the taxpaying citizens. In a society where the wealthy or wealthy businesses do not have to pay taxes, we are supposed to believe that those with money and influence are concerned with citizens that pay taxes? If the wealthy and powerful were concerned about the people at the bottom, they would pay taxes, which would in turn reduce taxes and people at the bottom would not have to pay as much.

Do not be fooled to think that individuals gaining wealth have taxpayers in mind when making money. If the CCA or other corporations want to help taxpayers and others, they should try doing what prison is designed for. These corporations should make it conducive so that prisoners can get an education and gain employment, which will decrease the chance of them returning back to prison. However, this will not work or happen, because that would be cutting into the profits, one of the main reasons for the design of the new prisons. Think about it.

The article also states, "Grasping the demographic make-up of today's prisons in the US and the history that produced this make-up (roughly 50% African-American, 35% Latino and 15% white), the privatization of prisons threatens to re-institute a link between race and commerce that has not been seen since the 1800s."[4]

In the 1980's, I watched the Arsenio Hall Show. During many of his shows, if not all of them, Arsenio asked questions about topics that were on his mind. He would say, "Here are things that make me say 'HMMMM'." Well, here is my Arsenio Hall moment. If Blacks are the minority in population, why is it that Blacks have the largest amount of people in the prison system? That is a question that makes you say "HMMMM". As stated previously, the psychological effects of being conditioned continues a cycle of return. The lack of understanding of the system and opportunities are fuels to the fire. The system needs to be evaluated to discover why there is a class of people that are not important enough to create changes within the system, so that the rate of prison decreases.

The system does need individuals to fuel the vehicle for the benefit of money. And according to statistics, Blacks are at the forefront of making money for the system when it comes to negative outcomes. It is like a return on investment. During the Christmas holiday sometimes, one does not like his/her gift. When this happens, an individual may rewrap the gift and give it to someone else. Thus it becomes the gift that keeps on giving. Similarly in the case of Black people, we are the gift that keeps on giving since slavery. We gave and continue to give many years of our lives to servitude from slavery until now. Slavery was hard time, hard labor. Offspring children from the blood lines of slaves dedicate hard labor and hard time behind prison walls and for what, the system. Please understand that by not making something of your life, you assist in the growth of other cultures by way of the cheap labor provided by prison work production.

I can't confirm or deny the facts around this statement; however I am told that many celebrities invest in private prison stocks. While writing this book, I had an interesting conversation with a good friend of mine who has invested stock in prisons. Although I love my friend dearly, he and I have very mixed views on various topics of investing in private prisons. From my standpoint I cannot see how any Blacks can invest in a system that profit from slave labor and slave benefits. My friend is about making money and ceasing an opportunity, which I cannot knock. To me, his investment is equivalent to supporting the high rate of Blacks being incarcerated, which helps destroy the Black communities/families. The mentality is get money by any means possible. We all do what we need to do; however, if I sell out, I have to get the hell out, meaning that this goes against my belief system.

Yes, private prisons have stock that one can invest in. On the website of the CCA, the stock ticker is so proudly and boldly visible, which is a smack in the face to a race that is derogated by the prison system. A Black person investing in stocks for prison is comparable to dog eat dog, cannibalism at its best. As the system conspires to condemn Blacks, we invest to support that system. As I stated earlier, everybody that is Black is not all Black or concerned about the problems within the Black communities.

With the push for profit, how much more effort will be dedicated to obtaining that profit? I have learned about judges who were sentenced to prison for locking up juveniles for the benefit of profit and greed. If one would Google "Judge Convicted in Pennsylvania kids for cash Scheme", the full story will be explained. Directly from the "Democracy Now", an article states, "A federal jury has found a former Pennsylvania judge guilty of participating in a so-called 'kids for cash' scheme, in which he received money in exchange for sending juvenile offenders to for-profit youth jails over the years."[5]

There are proposals in which the contractors for the prisons want to be backed by the government in order to be guaranteed a profit for the next twenty years at a 90% occupancy rate.[6]There is an article that suggests that contractors are suing states because they do not have the bodies in prison to make the money. When I say bodies, I am saying that there are enough Blacks locked away, because high prison rate, mean high number of Black/slaves in prison. The article that I am suggesting is called, "What?!? Private prisons suing states for millions if they do not stay full. The article states, "Private prisons in some states have language in their contracts that state if they fail below a certain percentage of capacity that the states must pay the private prisons millions of dollars, lest they face a lawsuit for millions more."[7] This means that the contractors want a guarantee that the prisons will be filled with prisoners, so that money will always be made. I say again, is it rehabilitation at state or profit? I do not see the prison system as something that people invest in because they want to rehabilitate individuals back into mainstream society. I see the prison system as a cash cow, where money is being made off of the disparity of people as well as our lack of thinking. Our lack of thinking is the commitment of crimes that do not pay. Notice that I did not say crime does not pay, but petty crime does not pay. Those that commit crimes that are illegal, money is made with no convictions? And again, I reference Michael Moore's *Capitalism: A Love Story*[8] for more understanding of legal corporate criminal activity.

Prison is a cash cow, a place where Blacks are the basis of the cash flow. Prisons earn money from each individual prisoner per day, per year. Before going onto my next point, I would like to point out that illegal immigrants have also become part of the money-making system as well. Illegal immigrants have been detained for what? Can you imagine explaining that their crime is only coming to this country? At one-point, Black people were classified as illegal immigrants of this country, forced over against our will, thus locked up in slavery. But I guess since Blacks have made this country billions of dollars with no return, I guess we are now legal.

Prisons also makes money from the phone calls made back home to family members. Money is needed to buy various items from the prison commissary. Bus rides and transportation to and from the prisons by family members is another means of money.

I am certain that I may not have covered all of the bases of how the prisons receive money. There is also a large amount of money generated by work, labor, and production. I call this the sweatshop factory. The U.S. Government Accountability Office defines a sweatshop as "an employer that violates more than one federal or state labor law governing minimum wage and overtime, etc., etc."[9] The thing that sticks out to me is that a sweatshop violates minimum wage laws. Hmm, so prisoners get paid what? From documentaries about prison and discussions with former prisoners, I find that prison work violates minimum wage laws. Who works for fifteen cents, twenty-nine cents, and up to five dollars an hour as a grown man or woman?

This kind of work is debt servitude, sharecropping, and all other accounts of what slavery is all about. The funny thing about this whole process of prisoners working for zero to minimum dollars per month is that, there are a large number of unemployed individuals within the free world (well free is an understatement). Jobs are being consumed by prisoners, when jobs can be given to those who are trying to make an honest living, feed their families, and avoid going to prison.

One question that no one seems to discuss or talk about is: if the prisoners are getting paid nothing to work, how much does the puppet master get paid for pulling all of the strings?

In all aspects, the pimp receives more of the money then the workers in the pimp game. If the payout is so low, how much money do the pimps in charge receive? So with all that has been discussed in this section, which side are you on? I say again, is prison rehabilitation or is it for profit?

"Understand that lack of education leads to lack of opportunity which fuels slavery within prison. The plot is being set to counteract freedom, where reduced education leads the children to become adults without hope and derogation and a pathway to prison."

Charles E. Hill III, M.S.

Chapter Sixteen

Military System

"If violence is wrong in America, violence is wrong abroad. If it is wrong to be violent defending Black women and Black children and Black babies and Black men, then it is wrong for America to draft us, and make us violent abroad in defense of her."[1]

-Malcolm X

This chapter is not meant to offend anyone that has served within any area of the armed forces or anyone who considers themselves patriotic. I commend those that serve or have served, the individuals who did what they felt was the right thing to do in their heart and in the eyes of America. I have my own opinion about the military and how we as Black folks are treated.

I find it interesting that years ago when we endured the high level of oppression, when we could not get jobs in America, where we were beaten and had dogs released on us in America, we were still either drafted or asked to fight for America. Muhammad Ali was correct when he said that he would not fight to destroy other poor and oppressed people when we have a fight on our hands in America. It was the law to be segregated in America, but acceptable to unite when we were needed to fight for America, to be used when needed. Yet once Blacks return from placing their lives on the line, Blacks needed to understand and know their place. You return back to the separation that you left, plus the possibility of not being able to obtain a job and/or benefits.

The movie *Dead Presidents* was a clear depiction of what could happen once a solider returns home from war. He or she is out of touch with the world and not able to adjust, which leads to additional depression/derogation. A deeper look is needed to understand what had happened. You live in America, oppressed and separated, and leave to fight in a war to defend the country that does not consider you equal. When you fight in the war, we are all equal. Upon returning to America, one does not return to anything different. The same inequalities that were experienced while serving in the war are now still present.

It is said that America is the greatest nation in the world. If this is true, being great does not mean that things are fair or equal for all. Though so great, should we not comment about the tragedies or the injustice that continues to occur generation after generation? To not comment would suggest that Blacks should shut up and take what is given, no matter what.

In returning back from the war, what chances and opportunities are there? The reasons for entering into the armed forces, due to the lack of opportunities, were to make a better way of life for yourself and family. Times have changed, and we are no long segregated as we were during the time period of World War II and the Vietnam War. Wait I am sorry, I said that completely wrong. We are not blatantly segregated as a people.

Prejudice, racism, and segregation still exist, just in different form. Therefore, as this nation continues to be divided, we appear to come together when there are problems with other nations, such as the aftermath of 9/11. There was a big push for the United States to come together and fight to conquer and destroy. I cannot say that I understand or fully know the true story behind 9/11 and the reason why weapons of mass destruction were never found. I do know this, whatever or whoever is the cause of the war, soldiers are trained to take orders from those in higher command, whether one agrees or disagrees. They take orders and follow commands that may not be safe for their health, life, or well-being.

In my opinion, everyone is not equipped to be a leader, a person that operates to make appropriate decisions under pressure and in pressure situations. For example, when I played sports in my time, there were players that were deemed the "leaders" of the team. During times when the game was on the line, the deemed leaders failed to step up when the pressure was at its highest level. I am certain that this may hold true at times during a pressure situation when fighting in war. I am certain that some leaders may not be equipped to handle the pressure and may give the wrong orders.

I will be the first to admit that I do not like being told what to do and/or to take orders, which is basically not having the ability to think for myself. The orders of someone else may not be in my best interest. If I was in charge and there were suspicious activities or possible bombing situations, would I investigate it myself? No way. I would send in a lower grade official to secure my safety. As I work through completing the process of this book, it is interesting how information seems to present itself. I had the privilege of viewing Nixon by Nixon. The documentary chronicled exactly what it is that I am discussing within this chapter. So allow me to explain.

During his term, Nixon, the President of the United States of America, gave orders to release bombs in Vietnam. The conflict was that the weather was bad and in climate where the pilots feared flying due to not being able to see. The President of the United States put pressure on the Chief of Staff to follow his orders. He wanted the land of Vietnam bombed at all cost no matter what. To carry out the orders would risk the safety of the pilots. So the orders recorded were for the pilots to implement the bombing or those in charge will lose their job/position. What this says to me is that there was no concern for the safety of the U.S. pilots as leadership behind the desk, in secure, safe, and not in the trenches, gave orders that were unsafe for others. Do understand that all orders are not good orders, nor are all orders in the best interest of security of each individual solider. And again, "for who, for what?"

I do not know every account or incident that has occurred; I have heard how veterans had to fight for benefits upon return with injuries from the war. Fight for benefits, hmm. I think I would be in a state of shock to have fought for what was declared a fight for freedom with me nearly losing my life, and in the end return home only to have to fight for health benefits and other resources to live. I do not understand how that is fair in any way. I would feel as though if I put my life on the line, I would need the red-carpet treatment. Instead, I witness old Vietnam War veterans with signs asking for food and money. I do not know all the details around each condition, but I see it enough to know that there is something wrong about what is going on.

I also remember the story surrounding Pat Tillman and often wonder how many other similar stories there are. For those who have never heard of Pat Tillman, Tillman was a professional football player that decided to leave the NFL and join the Army to fight the war in Afghanistan. First and foremost, I would like to send my personal regards to the Tillman family for what has happened around the entire circumstances of Tillman's death. I do not think that any family should have to endure what the Tillman family had to go through as a result of Tillman being killed by way of friendly fire, which is when soldiers on the same side shoot one another. The Pat Tillman story was an ugly display of lies and the covering up what was done incorrectly. The way that the military and government handled the case in regards to the Tillman family was just wrong and unjust. The documentary, *The Pat Tillman Story*, provides detailed information about what had taken place behind his experience in the military, his change in beliefs, circumstances behind his death, and the lies told surrounding his death. I encourage all to view the story and to determine what is fair and unjust. Just as the great saying goes, "Only God can judge me." So who am I to judge?

Chapter Seventeen

J. O. B. (Just Over Broke)

"The working man is a sucka."

-Sunny from "A Bronx Tale"

It is Sunday night and I have this pain in my stomach. Not because am sick with an illness, but I am sick of going to work. It will be the sta of the work week and I will attempt to muster the energy to complete all tasks and deadlines before the end of the week, just to come back t next week to do the same old...stuff. I strive to make it until Friday, when I can enjoy the quick moving two days off from work.

Damon Wayans performed a funny comedy skit about a man who asked to get a job as an actor with Wayans. When Damon Wayans asked the guy if he could act, the man replied yes because he acts as if he likes going to work every day.

Many of us are acting, acting as if we want to be at work and enjoy it, while there are individuals that will show by their actions that they hate the jobs they have obtained. While we all have to work to survive, I would bet that most individuals do not work from a passionate standpoint, but work just to keep the lights on (meaning food, shelter, and other basic needs). There are also others who work at a job that pays well, but they become a slave to the job or corporation.

I know friends who are in high-ranking positions at corporations and upon communicating with them; I get the sense that most are not happy. One friend shared how the boss calls her late at night, while she is at home to discuss work and projects that are due. *What??* I leave work to go home and forget about it until it is time for me to go back to work. This same individual told me that she did not clock out until 9 or 10 o'clock at night, just to return to work in a few hours.

The more one is paid, the more ownership and entitlement the job has over one's life. My free time is not for sell. I have always shared the idea that eight hours is too long to be at work on a daily basis, due to the fact that most of your day is gone. Here is the way that the corporate trap works. The American dream is to work for a company to receive stability with the idea of advancing higher in position. Some may advance, yet many will not, especially Blacks compared to other cultures. We all would like to work a job, build a career, obtain career security, and earn the money necessary to live comfortably, invest in stocks, and even save for retirement. Though we all would love that, however it is much easier to fantasize about the dream as opposed to obtaining the reality.

So in understanding how businesses and corporations work, do believe there is a different scale or ladder in how far Blacks will climb in terms of the majority of Blacks working in a corporate setting compared to other cultures. In undergraduate school, I learned about the glass ceiling in one of my business classes. The glass ceiling is defined as the unseen, yet unreachable barrier that keeps minorities and women from rising to the upper rungs of the corporate ladder; regardless of their qualifications or achievements.[2] Additionally, the fear of the Black man is always an issue and concern. Though the unconscious thoughts will never be admitted, Black men are bold and powerful just with are presence, verbalization, and at times the dialectic that we speak.

Now, I am not talking about Earl, Bo, or Jay-Jay from off the block. I am talking about a righteous Black man that has swag, confidence, and intelligence, who commands attention when he comes into a room. When I say man, this holds true for the Black woman as well. However, the Black man is feared more due to the bolder and brash demeanor that he possesses.

If you are Black, strong, and have an opinion that goes against the establishment, you have to go. If you are not in agreement with the establishment and speak your mind boldly, now you are deemed as the angry Black man. And when the business, job, or corporation wants you gone, believe me, you will be gone. Falsified write-ups suggesting that you are no longer efficient at your job will happen, although you have been efficient at the same job for "x" amount of years. The more writeups you receive, the easier it is for you to be fired. And if that does not work, there are always layoffs.

Then there is the classic, what I like to call the "times is up" layoff or "too old" layoff. These types of layoffs may come after one has devoted countless years of service to a job/career and had been promoted to the highest level the company will allow, yet he/she is then fired or laid off only for a younger individual to be hired. The younger individual will be hired at the same position with less pay. Yes, it happens. Then, the laid off individual will attempt to find another job, only to discover that he/she will not make the same (or almost the same) salary that was earned before.

The previous scenario does not hold true to everyone, but there are many cases in which this happens. So when there is the pressure of a mortgage, retirement, and children in college, how do you deal and cope with what has occurred? This is the thing: when you get out of school or begin to work, the American Dream is to obtain things that appear as if you are successful, have ownership of items that own you.

In the movie *Cadillac Records*[3], a singer named Wolf did not take cash advances and did not accept the given Cadillac automobile that all artists on the record label were provided. As I stated earlier, nothing is free. When a record label gives you something, believe you will pay it back. In the 1950's and 60's, a Cadillac was that time period's Bentley or top-notch Mercedes Benz. What people need to understand is that trap that is setup for you to shine. The trapping of America is for one to acquire things that they may not be able to afford or maintain for duration of time. These things gave one the appearance of status, but in a lot of cases that shining light is a mere illusion of what is really going on.

Getting back to the movie, in *Cadillac Records* singer Muddy Waters suggested that if Wolf stuck around long enough, he would receive a Cadillac like all the artists on Cadillac Records. Wolf banged on his old, rusty, battered truck and said, "I own it. It don't own me." I gave this example because there is a large number of individuals who are consumed and owned by what they believe will show that they are making it in the American system. Folks are swimming in debt over what is perceived to be the American Dream. I once heard an excerpt from George Carlin that stated, "They call it the American Dream, because you have to be sleep in order to believe." I call it the illusion. When you are working and lose your job, your former employer does not care that you have rent or a mortgage, bills, or mouths to feed. They do not care that you put in "x" amount of years and service at the j-o-b, thus kicked to the curb like they never knew you.

The fact of the matter is that many get used and played by a job after many years of service provided to a J-O-B. The working man is a sucka because the real trick is getting you to believe that your situation at work/job/career is stable. You work for a number of years or a certain time frame and become comfortable. Next, you begin to possess the things that show that you are successful, i.e. the car(s), house, etc. Then as years go by, you find that the rapid rate of money is somehow not enough. The cost of living begins to increase, but the salary and raises do not follow. Things that affect our lives such as gas, food, daycare, college tuition, interest rates, taxes, etc. all go up, but your income does not. Now you are expected to survive at the same rate.

You can start over by looking for another j-o-b. With the current economy and rapid rate of lay-offs, I say good luck. However, there is dependency of one's current job because in today's job market and current economy, finding another job or to gain financial advancement is slim to none. In no way am I suggesting that there are no additional opportunities; but additional opportunities are not easily obtainable.

I was once privileged to be introduced to a team of strong brothers and sisters within the Philadelphia prepaid legal system. Back in 2001 or so, these professional Black men and women were launching services. In the presentations, the men and women talked about wanting to break away from corporate America by way of network marketing. As a result, most of the presenters shared and discussed issues about corporate America that they disliked.

I recall someone sharing that a j-o-b or corporate employment was a form of oxygen or life support. That life support or oxygen is your bread and butter, your way of living.

I remember the message being strong, suggesting that if they pull the plug on you, your life support is taken. When a patient is on life support and the plug is pulled, what will happen? It is humorous to me that jobs suggest that it is proper to give employers a two-week notice (and in some cases a month notice) when leaving a job. Subsequently, when they want to get rid of you, they will fire you on the spot. Some companies are gangsta and make someone work the full day before they tell a person that he/she is fired or laid off.

Additionally, the individuals from the prepaid legal system discussed defining yourself and knowing your worth (know thy self). When one has a job interview, he/she will be asked what are they is looking for, meaning how much money does he/she desires to earn. I want to make a trillion dollars, but of course a trillion dollars is out of the range the job will pay. Though if you say you want to make $100,000 for a job that has a range of $40,000 to 50,000, you will be told no or that you are over qualified.

The actuality is that companies want to undercut you in order to obtain your services at the cheapest price you will accept. Also, many companies follow a budget in which there is no negotiation for salary. If most of us are honest, most of us are working under our value. Most jobs have an idea of what they are going to pay you. Understand that when the company gains profit, more money is paid out to the employers.

For example, teachers are in the social/human service field. In this field, one is helping and servicing lives. Human service is also assisting, building, and developing. Human service does not bring in a monetary profit. It is not a field where individuals obtain great financial gain. It is funny to me how other jobs and professions make more money than teachers. It is so apparent that teachers and/or other careers with similar value get treated as less than or not their worth. When the overall economy suffers, and money becomes tight, it is always the human service (not for profit) jobs that appear to get cut the most.

This is also the field where everything is consistently being changed and there are new, unnecessary regulations. There are individuals that sit behind a desk and think that changes need to be made usually make these regulations. Adversely, these are people that probably never worked within the field, have hands-on experience, or have been far removed from the front lines and are out of touch with what is going on. I call working in a field, working and interacting directly with individuals who face various economic, mental, and other major problems, as "working within the trenches". If these regulation changing individuals with power did work within the trenches, their work experience is probably outdated. They do not make things better, but in fact make it harder to perform basic duties. Due to the regulations set at the top, most bosses will make the job difficult to execute.

Rapper Mass Man in the song "Some Where In The World" shared, "All the things I do I don't get paid what I deserve/ and I feel my boss gets paid just to work my nerves/ who take his job too serious and he is just a jerk." Not just in the field of human services but in many jobs, the boss is usually a jerk. There are just some people in power or hold more powerful positions than others that should not be there. These are the individuals that use their position to be more than who they are in life. Have you ever met individuals who get hung up on titles and positions? I say, *who are you without it?*

In dating, I have noticed that people look at the title and credentials of an individual instead of looking at the person. The lesson is that one should look at the person without the titles and see who they are. Why? Because the credentials should not define whom that person is. And what happens when that person loses those credentials? You then would have to either deal with who that person is or discontinue communication with him/her. All in all, we need to evaluate our status of where we are and understand that a job is just that, a j-o-b situation.

If things were fair in the workforce, why would there be a need for affirmative action? Affirmative action is defined as "an active effort to improve the employment or educational opportunities of members of minority groups and women"[4]. Obviously there is a problem that has been identified in the equal employment for Blacks. A rule that most Blacks understand and know is that when there is an interview between Blacks and Whites, in many cases Blacks will lose out. I discussed earlier the game of Othello, where we are trapped inside the game because of the control of the corners and borders. Well, the job market is no different.

In most cases, in order to get ahead, we are told to go to school, get an education, and to find a job. In finding a job and/or landing a job, one enters the workforce working for whom? I do not think that most Blacks begin, establish a career, or retire from an entity of Black. The entities that I speak of are companies, corporations, or businesses that are established and controlled by other cultures. I am not stating that there are no Black companies and corporations. However on the large scale, the rules of employment, higher levels of executive positions, and the overall base of business are controlled by a game not meant for us. As a result of this control, we are populated in employment at a smaller rate than other cultures, thus the need for a course of action to work towards evening the playing field.

Does the course of action really even the playing field? Does it even give us a shot at keeping things close? One thing that comes to my mind is that the playing field with all of the laws, education, or anything else to "benefit" Blacks is never equal or fair. If you look deeper and open your eyes, you will see that the appearance is not what it seems such as having a Black figure as the President of the United States. President Obama could not get laws and bills passed because underneath it all, the control is not his. In 2010, I heard a Black woman share on the radio that she was not going to vote for President Obama even though she is a Democrat. Her reasoning was that she was not able to get a job and the President was not able to make the changes in four years as promised. Any intelligent individual would know that a four-year turnaround to an eight-year mess does not add up. Plus with the Republicans controlling the House of Representatives and Senate, the

President could not make any moves (pass laws) because he has no control.

Although the woman complained about not being able to get a job, she would have been out of work if the Republicans would have been in office by way of the presidency (2008). More Blacks would have lost more jobs. So do understand that it would have been worse if President Obama was not in office. But again this is where miseducation, being uninformed, tricknology, and unawareness hit us as Blacks.

Since companies were lacking diversity in Black employment, affirmative action was a law that was passed to increase the Black employment rate, particularly among large corporations. However, does the law provide a more equal field for Blacks? From my understanding, I thought affirmative action was for Blacks to obtain more jobs.

I recall a situation that occurred when I was a college student. I worked over the summer as a part-time employee in a factory making phone books. While working at the factory, I was told by other Blacks that worked full-time that the company was hit with a class action lawsuit. If I can remember, affirmative action did play apart in Blacks being hired in the local area and other areas where the company operated. I was told that the company who owned the plant was against hiring Blacks, meaning that Blacks were not given a chance or an opportunity to work. Thus, the company was hit with millions of dollars in lawsuits and fines. It was said to me that the company paid the fines instead of hiring Blacks at first.

Whether this story was actually true or not, it is still food for thought. And if it were not true, what would be the purpose of making up a story like that? Later, a gentleman who worked at the plant for years shared that he saw a massive hiring of Blacks, which I was a part of. Now, I guess the company realized that losing millions of dollars defeats the purpose of being in business. Therefore, I think I did benefit from affirmative action in one sense.

Affirmative action can be viewed as a victory without being an actual victory. We as Blacks, really have to discard the mindset that a few crumbs thrown our way should be considered eating or being feed.

On a larger scale, it would be in our interest to make and bake our own pie (American Pie), so that we can cut a bigger slice to eat. Affirmative action does not assure the right of being hired. It provides an opportunity, the equal opportunity of being able to interview for a job. Yes, being told that a situation is fair and equal does not mean that it is. So, you can be told that it is equal and fair, but realistically it is not. If things were fair and equal, Blacks would be employed at the same or slightly lower rate as other cultures.

When I shared with a co-worker that I am writing a book, she provided me with information regarding this exact topic. She shared that affirmative action is based on two parts, non-traditional and gender. This means that affirmative action hiring consists of employing workers of a classified minority base. Now let's take a look at how hiring Black women meets the guidelines within the law, in which tricknology strikes again.

There is an old saying that most have heard, "killing two birds with one stone." Hiring Black women can achieve two areas of the quota. A company can report diversity as hiring women, and then use the same women in the category of ethnicity, thus killing two birds. With the massive success of Black women in corporate companies, can one see where the theory may hold true?

Companies may believe that by hiring women, control is easier (not implying total control), pay a lower salary, and also meet the quota with fewer problems by way of challenging authority. With the increase in the number of Black women achieving a high level of success, I see where the Black family structure becomes divided. There are numerous Black women that feel as though a large number of Black men cannot match them as far as money and power is concerned. I believe that women, especially Black women, have overcome many mountains and hurdles in life. For this, I applaud and congratulate.

I believe that Black men and women equally work hard to achieve levels at the top. There are a lot of women who have succeeded because of a technicality in affirmative action, but will condemn the Black man because he has not achieved the same success. Now this is a conversation for another time, but affirmative action does provide access for some, even though the same opportunities may not be available to others. The access to work through affirmative action does have a limit and a cap in which companies and corporation can use to their advantage. Was it the intent of the law to assist a large number of Black/minorities to obtain employment? Whatever the intention, affirmative action has made the connection. Did it make things equal and fair? Are companies diverse to where culture dominance is not easily identified? Though the law assisted in giving some people opportunities, it also provides the companies with a cap on jobs that companies have to offer Blacks and other minorities. For example, not knowing the law but if the law requires 2% out of 100%, only 2% will achieve, a small percentage compared to the whole.

Basically, the individuals in these companies may be in a token position that keeps the company out of legal trouble. So do become aware and sharp to what is really going on.

Sometimes in losing a job, the battle is not yours. One can lose a job when he/she is not liked, not a part of the clique, or misunderstood by the employers or other employees. I experienced this first hand at one of my jobs when a woman, a Black woman at that, who wanted to exert her control over how I operated at my job. I had been at the same position for four years, yet this woman was new. I can see where she wanted to change a lot of things, as most people will do. Her changes were changes that did not fit within the job or even needed to be made. As she proposed her ideas, I opposed them. I also believed in working smarter not harder, as well as, *"if it ain't broke don't fix it."* And again, I worked at my site for four years no problems with things under control.

I will admit that there was one discussion, or disagreement, that we had where I could have taken the latter and agreed with her. Since I did not, there was an incident when she claimed she provided me with the necessary paperwork to be completed, when in fact she did not. As she plotted against me, emailing me her requests that I did not get, because the only access I had to e-mail was through my phone, which did not have consistent service within the building that I worked. So information was not received as needed. Plus, she and I had used texted messaging to communicate and she was at my site weekly, yet she failed to mention the paperwork to me. Due to the uncompleted paperwork, she requested to meet with me. She insisted, but I resisted because she was just at my site the previous day and had not spoken one word to me about any matters that were of importance. When I say that she did not speak one word to me, I mean just that. She avoided trying to see me because she already had it in her mind what it was that she wanted to do. So she was at my site a one day but yet a day later, there was a sudden urgency that we needed to meet the following day.

In meeting with her, I was given two write-ups at the same time. One was for not turning in the paperwork that she asked of me, although she never provided me with what was needed nor expressed this concern to me two days prior face-to-face at my site. The other write up was for being insubordinate.

Insubordinate! Now that is a strong and powerful word. Insubordinate means not submitting to authority or disobedient.[5]

I once heard Damon Dash give an interview, which I found very interesting. Damon Dash was the co-founder of Rockafella Records with Jay-Z during the 1990's. In this interview, was done after the company had folded or he was no longer a part of that business with Jay-Z, Dash elaborated how he challenged those that felt they were in power by way of their "titles." He explained that these individuals were made-up individuals, who had nothing to do with the industry and wanted to be more then what they were in terms of trying to give orders or make decisions that were unnecessary. This explanation stuck with me as when I thought about this person who wanted to exhibit her power, dominance, and control due to her title and position over me. Of course, I thought of her as a clown for her behaviors and actions.

Furthermore, the job was not that deep where I could not and did not obtain another. Plus, the fact that the money made at this J-O-B was not my only basis for making money. So knowing your worth and capabilities is always good.

Please understand that even though the unemployment rate is declining, the Black unemployment rate will always be higher. Now, why is that? I heard Al Sharpton on the radio speak about the public sector versus the private sector. The public sector contains the normal jobs that assist and help people for the benefit of improving lives and not for the benefit of money. These are typically teachers, mental health workers, public assistance jobs, etc. As stated previously, the jobs and funding that is usually cut when times get tough in the American economy. This is basically where a lot of Blacks fall in line in terms of employment, to help others.

Then there is the private sector, corporate and more conservative jobs. Unlike myself, these jobs are not for me. I say this because I am an outspoken Black man that does not see the need to compromise myself, views, and what I observe to be unfair or unjust. Therefore, the private sector is a place where I (and many others like me) do not fit. In many cases, these are the jobs that most Caucasians outweigh Blacks in numbers as well as many ambitious Blacks that see opportunity and can conform within this system. These are the jobs that seem more stable and have more of a financial backing. I view these jobs as more of selling your soul. As I recently stated, strong, Black, cultured, and outspoken do not mix in the corporate setting, in my opinion.

When I had a corporate job, it was perceived that I had to speak differently and act a certain way, which is the opposite of my outspoken and opinionated personality. There is a level of losing yourself and not speaking up when you are under the thumb of the corporation. For example, a strong Black Afro-Centric sister that works in corporate American with her own hair (no perm or chemicals, nor hair weave) is rare to see in the corporate setting. One must play the game, compromise in order to make the money. In a since shucking and jiving is what I would be doing as I had to suppress who I am for that type of job. What Blacks need to understand is the glass ceiling, meaning that there is a certain level Blacks will climb and face within the private sector. I will not say there are no Black CEOs in corporate companies, but the rare cases are the exception and then Afro-Centric expression is suppressed.

When I first began to write this section, I wanted to share the fact that in losing a job, one should not always feel threatened that he/she was not good enough or that they were the problem. As I would say throughout the years, when a job wants you gone, they will find a way to get rid of you. Sometimes, you can lose a job due to not being friends with various people in the workplace. You may stay to yourself, perform your duties, and go home. You may not want to hangout, allow people in your business, or want to get involved in the political aspect of the job.

In the news, there was a story about a woman who had been fired from her job because she was too attractive, and the boss did not want to cheat on his wife. What does a women's sexiness or looks have anything to do with her job performance? Therefore, understand that the overall loss of employment may not always be your fault or mistake.

So many of us work hard for a job or corporation and are underpaid for the work that we do. Upon working, one believed that if you work hard, remain honest, come to work on time, be respectful, etc., efforts will be noticed, and one would gain recognition and the money that comes with it. Countless people (Blacks) can say that is not the case. As companies try to cut back to save money, jobs are lost, and people become unemployed.

As a result of lost labor, the work is shifted amongst the other workers. So with your current workload, you now have additional tasks to complete, with no additional money/raise. When a company interviews you for a job, you are asked, "How do you fare with multitasking?" You agree that you can, because at an interview, you are answering yes to just about every question asked. Subsequently, as long as you work at that job, you will be put to the test. Yes, the company can cash in on you sharing that you could multi-task. As you complete your job and the additional work, you feel overworked and underpaid, basically not appreciated.

One day you decide to speak to your boss about the additional work and how this would be a good time to compensate you financially. As a child, I remember putting my fingers in my mouth, pulling and twisting a loose tooth in order to get that tooth out. Well, asking and attempting to get a raise is the same figuratively, a twist and pull process to get money from the company due to the burnout, monotony, and additional work provided.

On a side note, some companies are now in the process of making cutbacks. Medical benefits cut or reduced, which causes workers to basically foot medical bills because the insurance paid is depleted to the point of minimum benefits. So understand that the salary (if one gets that) and the benefit package (if one gets that also) are not as attractive as it was previous in previous years. But due to desperation, people needing a job will take it.

Once an individual has received this raise, the company feels as though since they are paying him/her more money, he or she can now do more work. The work will be more then what you were hired to do, more than what has been already assigned to you. Slavery is not only visible shackles, chains, and whips but also any other form of bondage.

What has also been known and discussed among us for a while is that once you get closer to retirement and your pension, the company will try to get rid of you, so that they will not have to pay out for retirement.

"The working man is a sucka," says to me that you work for nothing. It is an endless cycle of work to pay bills, to stay afloat, to make it to the next paycheck. There are a lot of people, good-hearted people that are working hard just to make ends meet. This means they are trying to keep it together financially to where the ends never meet, meaning the money is never enough.

"Being told broke is a joke but I ain't laughing much."
Mass Man, *Somewhere in the World*

Poverty is high and continues to rise. Due to the high rise in the cost of living, and minimum raises at work, affordable living seems to be an everyday struggle for the people that do not matter. The working man is a sucka, I say again, because we have been tricked to believe that the system is the designed method in which to live above the level of just making it. We were taught to get an education, and then graduate to get a job. And in many cases one does not feel as though they are making the money in which they desire to live. I once worked in sales and one of the top salesmen provided me with a message that assisted me in selling the product that we were selling. He said, "If you don't ask for the sale, you can't get the sale." With that being said, I made my own interpretation of the work/J-O-B situation. "If one is not making the money that one feels he or she deserves, has one put themselves in the roam to make the money that one wants to make?" The J-O-B fuels a J-O-B lifestyle, a J-O-B mentality and J-O-B way of living. To live under the current plan of action means what? The everyday common people live to be just that, *Just----Over--Broke*.

"How could one claim to be strong or a boss, as a strong man or woman for that matter, when lifestyle, way of living, and money made is controlled and depended by individuals or entities that controls your fate, where money can be taken at any time? "
-Charles E. Hill IIII, M.S.

Chapter Eighteen

Unification

Is unity just a word that is used in songs to sound good or is it a forgotten component of what we were striving for? If unity was ever needed, now is the time.
-Charles Hill III, M.S.

The basic definition of unity is "the state of being undivided or unbroken."[1] Because we are so broken and divided, our circumstances (negative impacts within our communities) are what they are today where we are individualized which keeps us from getting conditions changed for us. To better understand division, a discussion about slavery is used to illustrate the concept in more detail. The male slave was sent away from the family in order to divide it, which led to the family lacking its overall family unit. The plan and plot that was created for us was to not allow Blacks to become strong to have unity, as well as to strip away the history of the African culture so that Blacks would lack in having knowledge of self/self-worth.

The curse of Willie Lynch is well documented that there is great benefit in dividing the Black family. In understanding psychology of family dynamics, it is proven that two parents are needed to provide balance and a sense of stability for their children. Therefore please be aware that the negative plot for us continues to dwell within the Black community strongly to this day. For those who do not know about Willie Lynch, please research for a better understanding. Understand that Willie Lynch was a live figure in the days of slavery that preached the philosophy that Black men should be taken out of the homes to weaken the family unit. Though it is not specifically noted, but there had to have been an underlying thought to take the Black male slave away from his family to avoid unification in fear of rebellion.

Our leaders, strong leaders, were murdered because of what? Our leaders were intelligent enough to spark the interest and minds of the people in order for unity to be formed. Unification is a strong and powerful tool. Look at how Malcolm X, Dr. Martin Luther King Jr., and Huey Newton (Black Panthers) worked to rally the people to obtain better. Since the deaths of those individuals, we have not had the leadership that rallied the people to promote effective overall change. The leadership that is needed would guide us into the direction so that we could work together and work towards the things that we need and want.

Thus, in essence we are operating off of the ignorance as well as the tricknology that has been bestowed upon us from generation to generation. Instead of changing what has been placed in front of us, we are following the master's plan, which is for us to incite jealousy and division among us, as according to Willie Lynch. The plan was for Blacks to never organize and not formulate an agenda that could be beneficial.

I often wonder how conditions for Blacks get better. This question is directed to the Black people who have not lost touch with the struggle for Black, the individuals that can see that we as Blacks are still struggling. Those who have deemed themselves as successful by making money and living well should never forget one thing. Never forget that you are still Black. I say this because as many Blacks have achieved the America Dream of success, it is easy to forget about the struggle, if so many have not already forgotten at this point. Thus many well off Blacks from the financial aspect, have abandoned the struggle.

So I say again, how will things for us get better? Should we continue to do what we have always done, which is to complain about it or do nothing? The end result of not fighting for change means conditions will remain the same and things will continue to get worse. Therefore, it would be to our advantage to attempt

to make conditions better for the current generation and

futures ones.

As stated previously, the only way for things to get better is for

us to unify and to make them better. If you think about it, what

other groups or entities have made the conditions and

circumstances for Blacks better overall? In what way have things

ever been equal to where we have a piece of the American pie? We

need to wake up from the deception, plots, and restricted mind

control that have been placed on us for so many years.

When our great leaders talked about the circumstances,

ills, and conditions placed upon us to unite the people, the leaders

had to go. And why? The leaders provided a sense of pride,

knowledge, awareness, wisdom, and education. And with the

teaching and awareness provided by powerful leaders, there is an

awakening. This awakening allows people to stand up and fight for a

better way of life, which was and is not part of the overall plan for

Blacks in America. Why do you think that education was never

available for slaves? Why do you think that education has been so

diminished for us with the poorest of schools and fewer resources?

If you keep individuals deaf, dumb, and blind, it is easy to control

their minds with the elements of tricknology. That is why it is important for us to have guidance and rally together to work towards terms and benefits for ourselves. For example, we need better schools and resources; we need more jobs (independent businesses), and an overall shift in the negative statistics in America. And again, a shift and change cannot be accomplished without a strong unified united stance.

The basic definition of power is "the ability to do or act; capability of doing or accomplishing something." [2] Power is also defined as "great or marked ability to do or act; strength; might; force."[2] According to these definitions, when you look at power from the Black prospective, it appears as though there is none present within society. But if I can ask, has there ever been? Aside from the movements of Malcolm X, Dr. King, and the Panthers, where has power been exemplified within the Black community? I am not trying to convey that there have not been any obtained victories for Blacks. However the overall movement and shift to have power with respects to equality has never been available for Black America in America.

The lack of power for Blacks is evident. There is a plethora of topics that can be discussed where lack of power or fairness can be depicted. I choose to discuss one of the biggest acts of cheating, stealing, and robbery, which was the presidential selection of 2000. Notice that I did not say election, but selection.

A friend once told me that it is not an election; one does not get elected into office, but is selected. The average Joe, the common Black man, is not going to ever become president. Furthermore, the average affluent, rich, wealthy Black man will not become president either. The process of being president is a selected process in which Blacks do not fit.

A note that comes to mind: would President Obama have become president (or at least in the running) if the present economy would have been stable or if there was not as big of a mess as George Bush had left? If we had power or even a voice, why is it since the existence of the United States there has been one Black individual that has become president? And after all of the presidential elections, why is there a need for photo identification at the polls at this time? Tricknology.

Even though the 2000 election was unfairly won, there was nothing done to overrule the process. I believe that the election was rigged because in the very state that a sibling of former President George Bush was the governor, there were problems with the votes. This was such a blatant and bold act of "in your face." Then there was 9/11 and all the other mishaps of power under the direction of

George Bush. President Obama had not been in office as long as George Bush or provided the nation with the mistakes that George Bush had made, but he is disrespected. Why? President Obama cannot make a move without the press and/or others scrutinizing every move he makes. What this says to me is that he has no power, but more importantly, he has no power and can be disrespected because he is Black. Thus in one of the highest levels and positions of the United States of America, equality still plays as an issue. I discussed the selected election of 2000 because it was a clear and bold stance that showed power and how powerless we are.

Power does not happen without the force of togetherness. When you fight, you do not fight with an open hand; you fight with a solid closed fist. All five fingers work together to form a solid and strong fist, which is used to strike a blow. As the saying goes, there is strength in numbers and there is strength in togetherness as well.

It was a beautiful scene back in 1995 when Minister Lewis Farrakhan organized the Million Man March. The march showed strength in numbers as well as the power to unify in numbers. In my opinion, the march did not have any other meaning than a vast number of men coming together, but yet Black men did unite at least for one day. This also shows that we do want to come together for a beneficial cause to at least try to help ourselves.

I speak about unity and unification suggesting that if we do not help ourselves, who's going to help us or where will the help come from? The first thing that people say about Black folks and unity is that we cannot and will not stick together. I am not one hundred percent in agreement with that. Although it has been a long period of time since Blacks have united, it has shown and been proven that we can stick together when there is strong leadership present. I do not think that we should have a physical revolution, but there needs to be a fight, a fight for better. Fighting does not always mean to fight in a physical sense. Even if we do not fight physically, when we make progress and change, the physical fight is brought to our door step. Check the history of Dr. King, Malcolm X, and the Black Panthers to see different levels of fighting for better. As the Black Panthers were perceived by mainstream society as violent, they were indeed not violent, but yet the government imposed violence on them.   Malcolm X did not incite violence as he preached protecting yourself with violence when violence is brought to you, but yet killed violently. Dr. Martin Luther King Jr. preached nonviolence; violence was imposed on him and those that supported the cause.

Now I know what many people are thinking, how do we fight for better? Well like all great movements had, we need a leader. A leader will stand tall, discuss and explain the ideas that need to be conveyed to the people. President Barack Obama, in his position, cannot be that leader that will take us to the promise land. He cannot be that leader because of restrictions and situation. That resistance is illustrated by not being able to implement any policies for change because this country is still run and controlled by those who have always been in control.

I praise President Obama for being in the position and attempting to make change. Additionally, I commend President Obama for enduring all of the hate and criticism that he has received from every angle. Let me just say that I could not do it, to be in a public forum, allow people to take jabs and stabs at me, and to not fight back. If you back a dog in a corner, what choice does the dog have but to fight and bite back (not to reference anyone being a dog).

There is a fight in me that would not allow me to not fight back, to be nonviolent when attacked. The attacks on the President are mostly because people feel as though he can be attacked because he is Black.

We have to aspire to return to a place where we used to help and love one another. Too much of what Blacks represent to one another is hate, lies, deception, and defeat. I look at what we are doing to ourselves and it is not positive. The media reports Black on Black crime that we continue to engage in year after year. Why is that?

Black on Black crime is not just the events that occur in one section of the United States. It is an on-going condition that occurs all over the country. As long as I can remember, I have never heard of a story reported on the news concerning white on white crime or Asian on Asian crime. We are flashed all over the media being portrayed as savages and animals.

The funny yet sad part about it is that though this problem continues to remain year after year and generation after generation and nothing seems to be done about it. Of course, nothing is going to be done about it. Drugs, murder, courts, prison, etc., all fuel some kind of money for the system. In the overall grand scheme of things, when you are in the lower class or category that does not affect the overall operations of the system, you do not count. And when you do not unify to make changes, adverse conditions will continue to exist.

I hate the fact that gangs are formed to fuel murder, drugs, and violence. The gang organizations show that Black people can organize and fight a cause. Of course in my opinion, the activities and fight is for the wrongs of society in terms of what the gang stands for, but I do understand it. Our people need to understand that we are choosing to destroy our own communities when engaged in gang activities. When there were riots out of anger and rage, why do Blacks divert efforts to destroy the various neighborhoods in which they come from? It was interesting to me that when the verdict of Rodney King had been presented, Blacks would destroy their own neighborhoods, yet unified for a cause. Blacks felt as though there was an injustice by another race, yet the anger was directed towards the Black community. Very interesting. I am not suggesting that destruction is the way, but if you are Black, why destroy Black?

What we must get and understand is that the plot of our destruction is for the Black family to never achieve greatness as a family unit. Yes, there are Black families that live together and raise kids to be great. On the other hand, there are Black families that are together that more to destroy the children as opposed to assist in building a legacy. This type of toxic unification is not what we should strive for when looking at a model of what a Black family should be.

The presence of a strong man at home cannot be taken for granted. There is power in being a father, or let alone power within the Black family. Please understand the unity and strength in working together for the betterment of the next generation. Understand the benefit for your children and grand-children later on in life. As a man, you should not want your children to grow up without direction and guidance, only to be left in the world to find their own way. With statistics providing huge negatives for Blacks, I would say that the current plan of "I am on my own" is just not cutting it these days. One of our solutions is for the Black family to unify for unification and to strive for better as a unit.

We need to understand and become more aware of the things that have been kept away from us. Think about it. In our inception into the United States of America, we (as slaves) were not allowed to obtain education or knowledge of any kind beyond labor work. We were not allowed to vote or allowed to maintain the Black family due to the men being sent away from their families. If these things were kept away from Blacks back then, wouldn't it still considered negative to not have these things now?

Some would say that the Black family unit is highly dysfunctional, vastly divided, or do not exist at all. There are many reasons behind this way of thinking. I have my own thoughts and opinions on why. Whatever the reasons, this problem needs to be addressed so that unity is present among the Black family. As with the psychological barriers of teen pregnancy, jealously among Blacks, lack of education, not voting, going to prison, and the Black man not present in the household, all are traps of the master's plan. With this type of thinking, we fall right in line with what destroys and traps us. The things that keep us divided and stuck have become embedded within our existence.

I think that many of us have forgotten that there was a time in which we as Blacks were banned from being able to obtain an education and being able to vote. And when I say banned, I mean that individuals stuck together for a common goal, and many were killed for wanting to exercise our rights as Americans. Many years ago, strategic planning was used so that education and voting was never a privilege for Blacks. Through unity and the change of the times, we now have the right to education and voting. I say again, due to unification, we as Blacks now have the right to education and voting.

When I speak of Black people fighting for the cause, this also includes other cultures that have fought on the front line, debated politics of unfair, and injustice in America. The point about education and voting is that we fought against not being able to exercise our rights. Yet due to our conditioning, we fall in line with the master plan for us. There is a rebellion and direct defiance against exercising our "rights." I say "rights" because if we are not treated fair or equal, what "rights" do we have? Knowledge is power, and voting is power. Case in point, the primary elections in which most Blacks do not vote. As a result of this, President Obama cannot make any decisions. So do understand that all waves of voting are power.

Yet in order for things to change for a cause or agenda, unification is needed. And if we continue to stand divided means we continue to allow our fate to be dictated and determined by those who do not have a care or concern for us.

"United we stand, Divided we fall."

-Anonymous

Chapter Nineteen

Black Wall Street

"That's how the rich stay rich. Keep it in the family."

-Chris Tucker "Money Talks"[1]

When discussing resolution and resolve, there should be conversations about what to do regarding our communities. How can we improve and make improvements? Again I tend to think logically in terms of suggesting possibilities that will improve current situations.

There are various things that can be executed to turn things around within the Black communities, which are deemed the poorest in neighborhoods. Yet, Blacks are one of the biggest consumers. Spending among Blacks in this economy is high, which has become the cornerstone of other culture's elaborate lifestyles and survival. Allow me to explain.

One thing that I really do not understand (maybe because I am a man) is the hair weave for women, which is a strange phenomenon to me. When did it become unfavorable to misrepresent being Black? The hair industry keeps Blacks deadlocked out of the hair business, yet Black women support that.

The money is taken out of the Black community to assist other cultures in gaining a financial advantage, due to the large amounts of money that Black women spend on hair. On a side note, I have various thoughts around the adoption of hair weave. When women wear hair weave, I ask myself is there a sense of running away from, lack of acceptance, or not loving who they are? I also believe that there is just some laziness going on as well; some women just do not want to maintain the upkeep of their own hair. Either way, I sometimes observe that strong Black women live their lives in the manufactured trend of the representation of what Black women are supposed to emulate.

When we are lost and have no knowledge of who we are, we follow suit to what society dictates for us. I am not only speaking about Black women, I am also talking about Black men being lost as well. Hair weave has been accepted by Black men and consumed by the Black woman within our culture as large number of women avoid being natural, and men support this. The money being made is used to fuel profits for other cultures that are non-Black. Of course there is some consumption for the local beauty salons, merchants, etc. However, the money made is at the low end of what is being accumulated from the Black community.

What is interesting to me is that manufactured hair has been accepted and adopted as normal within our culture. I know women that have never been seen without hair weaves or wigs, all hair that is not natural. So is it safe to say that if one consumes most of the three hundred and sixty-five days in appearance of the hair weave, we can suggest that is who they are. I would say, a manufactured image of themselves, or not real to whom they are within the natural.

Everyone has insecurities and things that we do not like about ourselves, but what does it mean when one cannot reveal himself/herself without a mask or security? So if one does not like their appearance of their own hair, what are you saying about the state of loving Black and the fact that Black is beautiful? If Black is beautiful, then why cover Black hair with a culture that is not even Black? So in a sense, people are hiding who they are from the world to see. But what does it say when one cannot show the one that they claim to love who you are from inside and out? That poses the question of what other aspects of life one may be hiding within a relationship?

The basis of discussing hair weave is the consumption has

allowed other cultures to become wealthy and make us poorer. With the way we spend, the money should be spent within the communities to benefit our communities.

It is well documented and communicated that the dollar/money should circulate three times within the community before it leaves out. The hair weave industry consumes large sums of money that leaves our communities with no return.

Now think about it, if the money stays within a community, the community will prosper and continue to grow. In the movie *Money Talks*, Chris Tucker's character stated, "That's how the rich stay rich; keep it in the family."[1] I am in agreement of money staying in the communities, as in the case of Black Wall Street. Many Blacks do not know the history of Black Wall Street because the history books in school will never tell this story and most Blacks will not research the information.

Black Wall Street is about multimillionaire Blacks in the early 1900's. Of course, Black Wall is not part of American history (his-tory), but slavery continues to hit the pages of books of American history from generation to generation.

Before discussing Black Wall Street, allow me to further discuss money being circulated within the communities. The first thing that needs to be established is the quality and services of Black businesses.

When Black Wall Street was in operation, money could be circulated within the Black community because service, quality, and the needs of the people were met. Once again, there are Blacks that will and want to support a Black business, but service and quality tends to be so poor that people cannot support various Black businesses. The businesses that offer what the people want, continues to prosper.

Should the businesses within the Black communities that will not support the community be in the community? For example, I have nothing against other cultures conducting business in the Black communities but does that business support that community? Please note that our culture is studied to see how we spend money and what products we spend our money on. So while we are getting what we want, they are getting what they want, which is our money. Our money is taken out of our communities to never return, never to circulate within our communities again.

Why does this happen? It may be because one is jealous and does not desire to support other Black people, even though he/she is supporting someone of another culture. Another reason may be that

Blacks cannot organize in an effort to support our brothers and sisters out of love for being Black. Additionally, it is possible that we are too ignorant to understand that other cultures play us for fools and gain income, because of our lack of support for one another. Whatever the reasons may be, we are far from Black Wall Street. I refuse to believe that we cannot make efforts to move toward common goals as other cultures.

One day, I decided to cash my check in the center city section of Philadelphia. As in most cities, attempting to find parking downtown is the luck of the draw. The only available parking was the meters in Chinatown. As I got out of my car, I observed my surroundings to see a bank, stores, restaurants, and all other businesses that represented the Chinese culture. As I proceeded to my bank, I recalled seeing a section of Chinatown in Boston and heard about a similar location in New York. This inspired me to figure out exactly how many Chinatown locations exist within the United States. I used Google in my search and found that there are ten different states in which there where established Chinatown locations.

For those who do not know or who have not been to the place classified as Chinatown, allow me to explain. Chinatown is an area that represents the Chinese culture and has numerous

employment opportunities for people of that culture as well.
So do understand that money is being generated and circulated
for the benefit and purposes of one culture, Chinese.

As a thinker and processor of the things that affect us, I
began to think about this concept a little further. I also looked up
Jewish communities and yes, there are active Jewish communities
around the United States. Of course, I looked up Black or African
American communities to see if in fact we had some type of
community base, culture base, or profit base of our own. As I
researched, I am sad to say that I did not find any. So I say again,
profits and money is taken from Black communities and not returned
because Black entities and communities do not exist. For this reason,
we should be asking ourselves why.

Those who do not know or have never heard of Black Wall
Street, I encourage you to research it. Black Wall Street was an area
in northeast Oklahoma, around the city of Tulsa. This is where there
were several prominent Black businessmen with many of them
being multimillionaires.[2]

The area was a place that was separated from Whites and
where the dollar circulated to support Black businesses. As
people purchased and supported one another, whites would also

buy from Blacks. Due to the success within the community, a sense of pride and wealth was generated among Blacks. The dollar circulated to assist the community until riots in 1921 occurred, which were sparked by an alleged assault by a nineteen-year-old African-American male.

As I researched and explored the story through YouTube, it was stated that the young man stumbled onto the elevator, lost his balance, and accidentally touched a seventeen-year-old Caucasian young lady. Due to running into the girl, he was jailed and accused of assault.[3]

While the young man was in jail, a white mob declared a lynching of the young Black man for the accused actions. At the same time a Black mob confronted the situation. As a white man tried to disarm a Black man of a gun, a shot was fired into the air which sparked a continuous shooting match. From there, the White mob proceeded into the town of Greenwood, the location of Black Wall Street. The interpretation of the story is that Black men, women, and even children were not exempted from being killed. It was said that homes were raided and looted. To cover the tracks of the looting, homes and businesses were burned to the ground; in other words, a legal robbery.

Businesses were destroyed; reportedly six hundred successful businesses were lost. People at that time suggested that the ambush was planned because many white men, women, and children stood on the borders of the city and watched as Blacks were burned and lynched. I say again, Black men, women, and children were burned and lynched.

Black Wall Street is extremely important because it represents a time of unity and togetherness. Also this is the blueprint of the circulation of the Black dollar and how the wealth benefited the people. We need to revert back to what has worked for us in the past.

The perception of Black businesses in the eyes of many Blacks needs to be addressed. Often there is an understanding that the Black man or woman should provide the hookup when we purchase from a Black owned business. I have been guilty of this very thing myself. One walks into a Black business and expects your people to cut you a break, a hookup. Basically, what you are doing is taking food out of another Black person's mouth and diminishing the value of that business. If the person is not able to provide a discount, we talk them into doing so.

Furthermore, if we do not get what we want, we do not buy from them. Now what type of sense does that make? We rob our people, but support other cultures.

On the other hand, if you go into an Asian store, one will have little success in talking them down to obtain a discount, but will still support them. I can recall moments when I was short five cents or even a penny, some particular merchants would not allow me to purchase their item. We do not behave towards others the same way as we do to the Black man or woman by walking away. Why do we treat our people like that? How would a business person make money if everything is at a discount?

A friend of mine opened his own clothing store and provided me with an interesting story. He shared that he sold two shirts for thirty dollars each to a customer. When the customer paid for the shirts, my friend gave the man twenty out of the sixty dollars as a discount for the shirts. The guy looked at the owner and asked, "What are you doing?" The owner replied, "I am hooking you up." The customer said, "This is a business and you have to conduct business as business. We cannot go to big name stores and ask for a discount/hookup nor can we get a discount from an Asian store."

If you ask for a discount at an Asian owned store, they will look at you as if you are from outer space. So if we cannot cut corners with others cultures, why do we conspire to do it with our Black brothers and sisters who are trying to live prosper, earn, and survive?

The basis of discussing Black Wall Street was to first enlighten those that do not know about the history of prosperity of Blacks and the high success that Blacks achieved. Black Wall Street is a telling story, yet tragic. It is the rarely told story that depicts the fall, not failure of Black legacy that could still be in existence to this day. Black Wall Street could have been our development and expansion within other states, much like the Chinese and Jewish cultures. Unlike other cultures that have established culture and businesses, the Black advantages seem to be destroyed. So as I voice my concerns once again, I end this section quoting Lawrence Fishburne in Spike Lee's movie "*School Daze*", Black People, "WAAAAAAAAKKKKEEEE UUUUUUPPPP!!!!"[4]

Chapter Twenty

<u>Solutions</u>

"Too many of us have settled for living life comfortable in a discomfortable mind state and way of living."
                                        -Charles E. Hill III, M.S.

Throughout the process of writing this book, I have discussed the topics of this work with individuals. In discussions with various people, I experienced that mostly women were solely interested in solutions and not the problems. I continuously heard, "I am not interested in our problems, I am only interested in the solutions to our problems." Why is that?

When addressing a problem, it is better to dig into the root, which is the cause of the problem, and work from the inside/out in order to solve the problem. For instance, when one visits with a psychologist/therapist for various problems, therapeutic sessions do not begin with providing the solution only. The therapist, in order to be effective, must hear or research the problems, past and present. With that in mind, understand that in order to arrive at a solution, one must address the problems first.

Various behaviors or problems are not easily determined, thus neither are solutions. Although people drive cars, most do not know about repairing their car, but they can determine when something is wrong with it. The average individual will seek help from a mechanic who will research and diagnose the problem. In diagnosing the problem other concerns may be identified, which will fix the original problem as well as other problems. Concerns need to be diagnosed from the root and fixed from within or the same problems will be faced at a later time down the road.

As various problems from the past still exist in present day society for Blacks, do understand that this continues to happen as band aids have been placed on open wounds, which have not been properly diagnosed and treated appropriately. When trying to understand the problems within Black America, please start at the base and root to know that hidden wounds continue to reappear from one generation to the next.

One of the first things I think we need to do is stop the ignorance of our issues as if it does not exist, by definition of ignorance. Many Blacks are "comfortable," as if everything is fair. Some of us have achieved what we call success and no longer feel as though the struggle is ours anymore. So many become oblivious to Black issues until it directly affects their level of comfort, such as a job, a confrontation, or any other level of discomfort due to being Black.

When discussing the problems that plague Blacks, many people would ask, "What are the solutions to all of our problems?" I have heard on many occasions, "I am not interested in the past or our problems, but how do we move forward?"

At times I thought to myself, *what made me the individual that had the master plan, the keys to making it better for us as Blacks?* Have there ever been real solutions to our internal problems? If there had been solutions to our problems, then we would not be in the current position we are in today. We would be further along within the system then where we are. If one takes a look into the system and how it relates to us, one will recognize that each time we move forward, there are factors that come into play that pull us back.

I look at small things such as the Scholastic Aptitude Test (SAT). Once we as Blacks began to understand the test and lessen the scoring gap compared to other cultures, what happened? The test was changed. There were added components implemented in the test (such as an essay) and the scoring system changed. Why is that?

The SAT was created to show that one race is more dominate in intelligence over others. Therefore in understanding the reasons why we do not go further or run into many road blocks within society, do understand that prevented factors are present to prevent forward progress. Blacks have to work harder to maintain when changes are made from the standard that had been presented. Just as I spoke about the SAT test, when we figure out the test and shorten the gap of achievement, the test is changed. So when we make strides to go forward, we are knocked back.

When I look at the Black Panther movement and the unity that was formed among the people, history and research shows that the movement united the people for the betterment of Black people with positive solutions. Although the movement worked to be positive for Blacks, society deemed the organization negative as a whole. Many Blacks would say that the Panthers helped to move Blacks in another direction to move forward.

The end result was that many innocent people were murdered and sent to jail as society felt as though the Panthers were a threat to American society. That threat was to rally the people to think on a higher plain as a whole and to come together for the betterment of the people. Steps forward for Blacks always consist of steps being taken backwards. To assist in this regression, leaders were killed and sent to jail. Drugs were flooded within the Black community. Please check the history of J. Edgar Hoover's involvement and the stories behind the destruction of the Black Panther organization, as well as Malcolm X, and Dr. Martin Luther King Jr.

The information I am sharing can be read or researched. There are enough documentaries that have provided evidence of what taken place in our past history of destruction. The documentary "Bastards of the Party" shows how the Black Panther movement had been assassinated and the environment changed to pimps and drugs. So now we are no longer a collective unit, but divided as individuals.

The drug game is something that we need to fully understand. The money aspect of it should not be the focus, but the fact that the front-line and middle sellers are the ones being played for the fool. Think about it. You have the men and women at the top who supply the suppliers/wholesalers, who then supply a dealer that supplies other dealers. The ones at the middle and bottom of this chain assume the most risk through transaction, wars, and among other things. And those who are in the middle and at the bottom are? I ask this with respect to cultures.

The people at the top sit back and push the buttons with their hands clean of it all. Thus understand, for the drug problem in America to be stopped, you do not go after the people at the bottom; you go after the movers and the shakers, the individuals that make things happen. But just like most things in America, money makes the world go round, so your life is expendable in order to keep others rich. Drug use and drug dealing was another means that tore our communities apart. Please understand that drugs were and still are another way to keep us divided.

We would be further along if we would have continued to receive the guidance and wisdom from our great leaders, who were murdered. We had strong and powerful leaders, such as Malcolm X, Dr. Martin Luther King, Marcus Garvey, and Huey Newton (and the Black Panther movement). These individuals' and organizations' concepts may have been oblivious to many whom are not Black. I say this because their messages were misinterpreted as negative by mainstream society. Where we would have had unity with leadership, we now have confusion, disorganization, disillusion, separation, no hope, and derogation.

One of the first solutions to help Blacks move forward is to have leadership, guidance, and an agenda. We need an understanding of the system. There needs to be a re-education of what it is that we are doing and where is it that we need to go. There needs to be education on family values, education on how to work within the system as well as work outside of the system. There should be education (or better yet development) about divine knowledge, wisdom, intelligence, and about how to be great. Too many of us are taught how to be average or below average by way of formal standardized education or not to receive any education at all. As society is in an infinite state of change, many are waking up to see that going to school to get a good job/career is just not the way. Obtaining this way of living is enduring living life average or below average in terms of finance. So many of us have untapped talents that go to waste. I think that many of us do not look at or try to work with our gifts until we figure that the path of working for someone else does not provide us with the standard of living that one wants to obtain. Case in point, I tapped into writing on a more serious level after understanding that my lifestyle will continue to be average working in the J-O-B realm.

There needs to be an understanding about how to raise children and economics (interest, saving, etc.). Black folks need to understand beforehand the importance of being a mother and father to understand all other negative forces among Blacks that destroy the family unit. We need to gain knowledge on the importance of a healthy, stable household, where there is a mother and father to raise great children. Parents need to understand that having children is a sacrifice; where the children obtain and receive nurturing, security, stability, and just about everything else that is needed so that they can grow and prosper.

Blacks need to become aware of curses on their families and wake-up to erase the unconscious hate and jealousy of and among Blacks. I spoke earlier about the impact of Willie Lynch and how he gave seminars to educate whites on how to control Blacks mentally and physically. Ladies and gentlemen, it is now

2015 and we still have to talk about a man from the 1700's. Why? Because you cannot place a band-aid on an open scar and think that it will heal without repercussions. The seminars addressed the dividing and conquering of Black men and Black women. One of the ways to do so was by turning light skin against dark thus house nigga versus field nigga. To this day there is still the mentality of house and field, which keeps the jealousy going. One will hate the fact that another Black individual has, and he/she does not. Why is this?

I cannot see the idea of doing well financially, only to look down at poor Blacks and people at the bottom. Black people are Black people, poor or well off. However ignorance is ignorance, rich or poor. The poor are looked down on from those rich because one has not acquired what someone else has. Instead of looking and teasing, people should assist in lifting up brothers and sisters. Now this lift does not always mean financial. I applaud MC Hammer for employing and allowing other Blacks to benefit from his success from a financial standpoint in the mid-1990s, but do not forfeit all of your wealth for the benefit of others.

More people that have the finances to assist should do so; assist as they can. What I mean by this is collective financial efforts can change lives and communities from poverty. Oprah Winfrey started a school in Africa. While I applaud efforts to assist and help Blacks, there are many Black schools in the United States that are suffering. Unfortunately, many who are successful do not assist poor communities with help as needed and why is that? There are a plethora of rappers, actors, athletes, and other notable figures that come from the hood and do not contribute back to the hood in which they came from. For me that is not keeping it real, but I could be the only one who feels this way.

Again, I will say that I do not have the solutions to all of our problems. I will say that I have logical reasoning skills that are rational to the problems that we have. I do not want to think or believe that the future is bleak, and changes cannot be made. I have felt for a long time that we need the necessary leadership that I spoke of earlier. The late great Tupac shared that all our leaders die by murder and never from natural causes. Why is that? The motivation of Blacks to do more, to be more, to think further, why is that a crime? Why is murder or a stay in the penitentiary the path for our strong Black leaders, and why has there been a lack of Black leadership?

If we research and check our history, one would find that those who motivated the people, Black people to another level, were murdered. I came across the killings of the Black Panther party, in which the Panthers in self-defense fired one shot in defense as others in the home had been shot and killed by the police. Though evidence showed that the Panthers were not at fault for the attacks, the law justified these killings as legal. If we did not stand up for injustice of Blacks, then tragedies will continue to increase. Just recently the police shot a man who was innocent of no crime, but yet a Black life has been taken. I think that it is strange how a trained officer of the law can murder an individual and receive a slap on the wrist (minimum jail sentence or no sentence at all), but if an ordinary citizen kills a cop, the citizen will spend life behind bars, or worse, receive the death penalty. We have to fight and stand up for our justice and injustice that plagues our communities. When I say justice, I am talking about as much of the justice that we can receive that is fair and in our favor, but this system was (and is) not designed for our benefit. This is quite obvious by the conditions still imposed on us, the large gap in disparity, the gap in prison, gap in education, and all other negative aspects in America, as well as the continued fight for us in terms of equality.

What I would like people to focus on is that we need to rally together for our causes that serve our benefit and purpose. As with the election of 2012, we should always rally in numbers at the polls in order to see whom we like to be voted into high office. All in all, we need elected leaders (not the president) to guide us, someone who has strong views, strong values, and an agenda for how we can go further to climb the mountains of life. This or these individuals will need to be able to accept being torn and beat down by the media, who assassinates one's character, case in point the treatment of President Barack Obama.

The media and others have tried to drag the President through the mud, his name that is. I am not saying that these potential leaders should have a past with no problems. I am not particularly concerned about the past, because a person that is rehabilitated is a person who has gone through experiences and has learned from them.

My pastor even preached that he used and sold drugs in his past life, yet he is a man of God and an inspiring preacher to this day. Malcolm X was a thug, a former drug dealer that had been to jail. Huey Newton was a thug that spent time in jail before and during the Black Panthers movement. Dr. Martin Luther King Jr.

even spent time in jail, as did Nelson Mandela. In the case of Mandela and Dr. King, jail time served was not direct results of criminal acts as much as racism and rallying the people. Therefore, the past behavior of an individual is not nearly as important as what an individual can bring to the table as a leader.

To be clear, mild behavior can be overlooked, but serious or extreme behavior will not gain creditability with the people. This person or individuals has to have the morals and beliefs about Blacks progressing and should also have the ability to provide a plan of organization and unity among the people.

A leader has to understand that there will be infiltration and deception by his or her own people. To understand this point better, watch "Belly," a movie that clearly explains how Blacks are used to get close to other Blacks only to tear them down. The enemy will always find some individuals on the inside to cause disruption and confusion within the ranks of power. Some examples of this are COINTELPRO, with the Black Panthers and the government using the US Organization (another Black movement similar but different then the Black Panthers) to incite conflict with the Black Panthers organization. For those who are not familiar with what happened in the past, please research.

Both were fighters for equality in their own way, yet the government used the two to war against one another, thus another case of the Willie Lynch, thus divide and conquer.

When I discuss and speak about unity, there are many Facets of Blacks sticking together. Blacks as a whole, need to stick together for the overall goal of moving further. To move forward means for Blacks to have better communities, schools, families, and overall quality of life. When I say this, I am not just talking about individuality where one makes it out of the worst conditions and forgets about all others. Successful Blacks should work to assist other Blacks on becoming successful, like the motto "Each one, teach one". The problem with success is that many will turn their nose up or down at those who have not achieved the same level and we need to stop this backwards mentality.

For those who feel as though we as Blacks can never stick together, your minds are already defeated, but I do understand. We as Blacks have become divided and have a lack of togetherness. Families are not even together in present society. It is also very easy to not stick together for equality when you are living comfortably. Too many of us are just overly comfortable at this time or living life comfortable in an uncomfortable state, and do not feel as though actions need to be taken because problems are not directly at one's door step. Also, if those comfortable in success become involved and get your hands dirty, you are now discomforted in your current lifestyle. I bet that many who are doing well (i.e., celebrities) fear how others will view them or that they will lose what they have. In my opinion, real is real. If you are for the cause, you are for the cause no matter what others may think.

Some Blacks have forgotten the history of Blacks needing one another to improve situations for Blacks. If one thinks for a minute, many that are successful are living life comfortably because others have fought for the freedom of current day society. So in essence why not pay it forward in some way? More unity was formed in previous generations because we had nothing. This is why it is important to know one's history and not just his-story that is taught in school. Not knowing your history keeps you deaf, dumb, and blind, as well as ignorant. It bothers me when people say that they are not concerned about what has happened in the past. History is important because it keeps people aware of what has taken place in the past, what worked for a period of time, and what did not work.

When I speak of organizing with an agenda, I am not talking about fighting physically against the system. History will show that a physical fight will never be won. There were things that were done to assist in making a number of conditions better that allowed some Blacks to be where they are today, which is progressive but not in the overall sense for Blacks. So if Blacks have stuck together for various opportunities, why disconnect? Again, unification can take on different forms. Communities can band together to make the community better and to put the politicians in office that will get things done with the Black agenda in mind. Politicians come to our communities for our support and votes; therefore we should be able to cash in on our votes, as we need. That can only be accomplished when we ban together with consistent applied pressure and in numbers to get what we need or want. Again ban together to elect individuals that will truly fight for the benefit of Black, the same agenda of those in office that fight against the benefit for Blacks.

Remember the saying, "It takes a village to raise a child."? Presently, the village has turned into areas where a village is a foreign concept. In the past if a neighbor, teacher, or authority figure reported to the parent about disrespect or inappropriate behavior by their children, the parent would implement the necessary discipline. In fact, the child would fear the wrath of the parent finding out. Also, the authority figure (teacher, neighbor, etc.) provided discipline to the child and then the parent would support the discipline provided and would implement their own form of discipline as well.

Currently, parents may not even provide discipline or interventions, so the children do not fear any consequences. I have observed how parents will take the side of their children when their child is wrong and out of line behaviorally. Children can be disrespectful, knowing that there will be no real consequences for their behavior. Parents need to realize that discipline, rules, and boundaries should be established early and continuously in a child's life. Although a single parent can perform this practice, a strong family unit can aide in avoiding many problems for the children.

It is time for the Black family structure (whether together or not) to take care of the children. Adults need to put emotions and differences aside with the purpose of doing what is right to benefit the children. In my opinion, I do not believe that the court system (i.e., child support, custody) needs to be involved in your family's business. I believe that two responsible adults need to be able to work out differences and create arrangements. I do agree with the decision of the courts being involved when the man or woman does not provide any type of support to their children. Then too, more thought and planning need to take place by way of not having unwanted children and to choose a mate with compatible value systems and beliefs.

Along the lines of unity, both parents should work together to provide stability for their children. Both parents need to provide wisdom, knowledge, support, and education. Additionally, we need to break the curse or mentality of random reproduction. When you decide to produce a child or children voluntarily or involuntarily, one's life must change. The late-night partying and all other frequent behaviors that do not benefit the child need to change. It is now time to make sacrifices that will benefit your children. In providing benefits for children, I wonder why we continue to allow this inferior education from generation to generation. In just about every predominately Black or poor environment, the schools are the worst. In just about every city across the country, there is less for Blacks in the Black communities. There is less money, resources, and the conditions are dilapidated. Schools have not been remodeled since their inception. This is where we fall for the same trick year after year, generation after generation. We accept what is told to us, that there is no money in the budget to fix, repair, remodel, or provide opportunities. Think about it; every state that has had reduced education, funding continues to have the same budget problems to where the poor cannot get the same caliber of education. It is funny how there is no money for educational opportunities for Blacks, but there are large sums of money being spent to build new prisons. These prisons are built for whom? Additionally, if we do not unit and fight, things will continue as they are and most likely become worse.

As illustrated earlier, elected officials are taking money away from education and the same money is being used for things that do not benefit Blacks or people who are poor. This type of wrong-doing is becoming more direct and blatant. Why does this continue to happen? The answer to that is there is no unity or unification that allows us to fight for injustices. Hence, when are we going to stand up to get better for our children and future generations?

Other notable suggestions in attempting to make productive changes for Blacks are to think outside the box and get out of the systematic way of thinking. People should be honest and admit that the system is not working for us as a whole. The system is and was never designed with us in mind. If it was or if things were better for us, we would have progressed further then we have. The economic gap would not always be so widespread. The number of Blacks in prison would not be such a disparity. Unemployment and all other negative aspects for Blacks would not be so high. I too, still need to clear my mind of what I have been brainwashed into thinking and believing. We need to understand as much as possible about the system, the operation, laws, finance, and anything else that benefits or destroys.

The knowledge that is obtained and learned should always be shared and taught to others, especially the youth. Young people must be taught the beliefs, values, and operations of the system so that unnecessary steps and pitfalls can be avoided. Each one, teach one. I try to provide as much wisdom as I can to adults and especially young people that I encounter in order to begin the process of them understanding what is going on in this world. I strive to turn on the light and get the wheels churning in their brains as much as I can as they are still young.

During a recent conversation with my nephew, I shared information that can assist him as he grows and matures. I witnessed his facial expressions that showed he was stunned by our conversations, as he verbally agreed that he is aware of some things we discussed. I shared that some people are mentally dead, explaining that people are not thinking, not knowledgeable, have no understanding, or just oblivious (ignoring or ignorant) to the tricknology going on around them.

I also explained to him what it is to have a third, all-seeing eye. For those who do not know what the third eye is, I encourage researching and reading up on it. The third eye is the invisible eye between your two eyes that assists you in seeing what is unseen. Basically, when one is overly aware of what is going on, I would classify that as a light in one's brain where many have a light that is off. When your third eye is open, your light is brighter so that you are able to see more than the average person. I shared with my nephew that when your third eye is open, it keeps you sharp, alert, focused, and aware. I explained that assistance of your third eye is like entering into a room and becoming aware and recognizing that danger is among you. I was proud to see him attentive, and in tuned with the knowledge I shared with him. Therefore, teaching and learning needs to take place.

In regard to thinking outside the box, I have to train myself to step away from traditional ways of thinking also. Slaves were trained to think systematically to work and perform duties as the system suggested. The majority of people in society think systematically by way of systematic training.

I was taught to go to school, get a job, and work for someone else. This is the safe route in life, where life becomes the everyday struggle. If most of us will be honest, this route has been the path of struggle and compromise. Although there needs to be an understanding of the system by way of education, I do not agree with doing exactly what the system has set for our lives. Money is paid for education and money is owed. Jobs are gained, and jobs are lost. Most jobs do not provide the lifestyle that will result in comfortably in what has been deemed the "American Dream." As times change, jobs do not change with the times. The cost of living increases and salaries either decrease or remain the same. Hence the dream is now the illusion.

Mind control is the way in which we conform to a way of thinking. For example, as slaves we were not allowed to become educated, we were in prison which is slavery, not allowed to vote, had multiple children with no fathers present, and worked for others (whom were non-Blacks). We were taught to hate one another and to not be unified. As I said before, we fall right in line with the plan of mind control. Now that the organized plot of slavery is over (as we are in present day society), the mental mind and slave mentalities still exist. We still receive less and insufficient education, a high rate of Blacks in the prison system, fathers are not in the homes, work for other cultures that are not Black, and we rarely vote (though current elections have increased among the Black vote).

The lack of obtaining education or the wide gap in achievement also falls right into the plan set for us. By Blacks remaining in prison (allowing economic gain for others) as well as our fathers not providing a strong family structure in the home, these are also areas that we have fell in line with. When thinking about solutions, I think that one of the biggest things to do is to overcome the mind control of our problems. We need to fully understand the things that keep us confined mentally as slaves. At this point in our lives, many of us still have the slave mentality. The sad part about it is that so many do not even know it.

As I recently watched the movie "Malcolm X", I remember

how they talked about the house and field nigga. Denzel Washington played the part of Malcolm X, illustrating how the house nigga lived better, ate better than the slaves in the field. When the house caught on fire, the house nigga was the first to put out the blaze. When the slave master was sick, the house nigga suggested that he (the slave) was also sick. When the field nigga suggested that they run away to a better place, the house nigga shared what better place is there then where they are. I can feel that passage because there is a lot of shucking and jiving going on to this day. The mentality of individuals whom have made it as a Black men and women are partial to the overall success of the Black race. I give people credit for those whom have made a way for themselves and their families. However, if there is no support to uplift other Black men and women in America, what are you really saying? The movement by high profiled Blacks in America to assist other Blacks is nothing to brag about if there is nothing being done. Again one must choose and pick a side, house or field.

Some of the things that I do not do are watch the news, conform to other forms of media, and partake in entertainment that promotes, in my opinion, lies, bias, and propaganda.

Propaganda is defined as the spreading of ideas, information, or rumor for the purpose of helping or injuring an institution, a cause, or a person. Propaganda is also ideas, facts, or allegations spread deliberately to further one's cause or to damage an opposing cause.[1] The news media reports propaganda daily by way of Black on Black crime. How is that all so evident? This is clearly a way for a picture to be painted that Blacks hate one another. Are Blacks the only race of people whom have committed a crime against one another? As I shared earlier, I never hear about white on white or Asian on Asian crime.

Music also conspires to fall into that gray area that is a form of mind control. People do not realize how their favorite artists and actors are used to direct subliminal thinking. When I was younger, rap music had many different genres in which to be entertained. There were party rappers, gangster rappers, and intellectually concise rappers. When rap music first started it was formulated by the innovation of the culture, a natural occurrence of events. Once it was understood that rap music was not a fade and was here to stay, those with money entered into the industry. So as those with the money and are not from the culture, control the products being put out. Most artists or rap music on the radio is commercial and watered down.

Rap music and artist these days are more of a manufactured image of today's culture now called hip hop. I have no idea where the present state of rap music (hip hop culture) is and is going. Men are wearing skinny-legged jeans, singing like an R&B singer, and everything is about money, money, and money. "That's why whenever there is problems and conflict/ we instantly act like little devilish monsters/ since our culture is so damn demonic/ only s*** that we honor/ is Drugs, money, b*****, and violence!!!!!"

-Mass Awakening, "Subconscious Monsters"

We need to organize and unite, work together to create a plan that will benefit us. We have been plotted on and now we have reduced education, reduced opportunities, and pathways of life that lead to the penitentiary. I believe that we got lucky in this past election, having the individual in office that we desired. He was the person that would not make the economic situation of the poor worse than the individuals that do not care anything about us. Thus without his lack of power in his position, conditions are still controlled with the people we did not want in office. Therefore in the future, we need to have elected officials that will support and benefit us at the bottom of the food chain. Why is it that we have never had an elected official that has supported change and benefits for Blacks or all others in the same socioeconomic conditions? As there has never been an elected official to benefit poor people, wouldn't now be the time?

We need to form an agenda before that magical day when things become so far out of line that it may be almost impossible to recover from. Situations are not appearing to improve, but becoming worst in the overall state of Blacks.

People need to realize that the building of more prisons will mean more decreased opportunities and education in order for us not to become productive members of society. In prison, we will become a number and income by way of our names in jail. One of our solutions has to counteract the prison plan or else many of our children, grandchildren, and so on will cross paths in detention, prison, and confinement.

More young people need to be informed that life is about making choices to be different, to step outside of the system and become leaders and owners. I learned that the Monarch schools are schools that teach children with an open way of learning. The schools allow students to teach themselves and each other. As a result, the students learn differently with an open and free mindset. I would say they
learn with a non-traditional way of thinking. I believe that a lot of

our children are taught to be average by way of being trained to go to school, get an education, then to work for someone else. Due to the way most Blacks grow up in their environments, they are taught to be less than average by way of the reduction of the tools necessary to think further then where they are. This occurs not only with the teaching, but the overall census and consciousness that projects a less than average mentality.

Leaders and great people need to be cultivated, elevated, and most importantly join in the game. I refuse to believe that only strong leadership ended at the end of the Panther movement. We need to revert back to some of the old teachings and positions of our ancestors of our past. A good example of leadership and ownership was Black Wall Street. Not only did Black Wall Street exemplify leadership and ownership, but the community also having pride and unity. Please understand that the point of viable productivity had come full circle. The things that tear us down and separates us need to be first recognized and depleted from our way of thinking and living. We have to be smart enough to see the game, understand the game, and not just be pawns that systematically box us in. One needs to be aware of one's moves and actions to not be controlled by the puppet master. The puppet master can be anyone or anything that keeps you mentally enslaved.

Due to the conditioning of our minds and actions, we need a reprogramming to delete what we have been taught throughout the years. Adults need to re-evaluate their lives and recognize the curse that has been bestowed onto them. Then we need to determine what curse we have placed on our children and the next generations.

I will admit that a curse in my family that I strived to break was not producing children early in life, or to product children by way of a mistake. When I say mistake, I am talking about the lack of planning to have a child. I decided that I would not do what my siblings, relatives, and friends have continued to do from generation to generation. I am not suggesting disrespect to anyone who has taken that path in life, but I am just stating that I wanted to be different and live my life outside of the norm. So as much as I can, I talk to young people and suggest to them that they also do not have to live within a box. I shared that you do not have to be a robot like a lot of other people in this world, doing what you have been trained to do and have seen for the duration of your life. Although I have succeeded in breaking that family curse, there are still somethings in my life I still need to clean out from the robotic, trained, systematic way of thinking.

We need to reprogram ourselves so that we can do better. I often suggest providing seeds to the youth through knowledge, wisdom, and a different understanding of how things are done. I chose the youth because the youth represents seeds of life. If provided the appropriate necessities, the seeds will grow and blossom into something powerful and great. Additionally, the youth need to begin making arrangements for their futures at an early age because the world is not too forgiving of mistakes being made when you are Black. The system will just lock you away in the newly renovated detention centers and/or prisons which those in power profit from. The youth need to be aware and empowered to think beyond their current situations.

Adults can and need to make changes as well. Adults can replant seeds or cultivate the ones that have been previously planted. It is never too late to sharpen your mind, body, and soul. We need a different path and direction in where we are going. We need love, happiness, and togetherness in working towards an agenda that works towards our benefit.

Ladies and gentlemen, I could elaborate on so much more about our problems and what we can do to make productive changes. I started this process desiring to enlighten individuals about what is going on with us as Blacks as many of us do not focus to think about what is really going on. I believe that I have provided enough information on the things that affect us. Logical reasoning was used and provided regarding improvements we can make for ourselves. Clear-cut solution to our problems is not an easy feat for any man or woman.

I do not believe that our problems can be solved easily through quick, fast solutions. As I researched when we as Blacks were successful, there were some things done that worked for our benefit. This is why I continue discussing unification and unity. When we come together with a viable agenda, things can be done to benefit us. Black folks need to understand that we are powerful and that we are stronger then we think. Why do you think that movements that have united the people had to be terminated? Do understand that the strength in numbers conquers all. The slave like mentality keeps us conquered and divided. I know many people will still ask, how can we create unity? How do we organize? What are our plans and agenda? So many questions and not enough answers.

No one knows the solutions to all our problems; I do know that if we continue to stand still and continue to do nothing, we will continue to fall victim to whatever comes down the pike for us. We will continue to be controlled like puppets and slaves, thus increasing slavery by way of prison. As an old adage goes, *if you do not stand for something, you will fall for anything.* We all cannot sit on the sidelines and cheer people on or always wait for instruction. Get in the game and participate yourself.

Many people ask me what are the solutions and what will "I" do. My question to you is, "What are your solutions and your contributions? Are you way up in the stands, or are you in the game fighting for a victory as well?"

Recommended Readings

The Mis-Education of a Negro

The Auto-Biography of Assata Shakur

The Huey P. Newton Reader

Breaking The Curse Of The Willie Lynch

From The Browder Files: 22 Essays Of An African American Experience

Think and Grow Rich

Think and Grow Rich (Audio)

Recommended Documentaries

Bastards of the Party

Booker's Place: A Mississippi Story   The

Pruitt Igoe Myth

Aftershock of the Civil War

The One Percent

Black Wall Street

The Koch Brothers Exposed

Dark Legacy

Central Park 5

NOTES

Introduction

1. http://en.wikiquote.org/wiki/Tupac_Shakur

2. F. Gary Gray. 26 April 1995. Friday: New Line Cinema. USA.

Chapter 1

1. http://www.ask.com/question/what-is-generation-curses

2. Antoine Fuqua, & Cle Sloan. April 23, 2005. Bastards of the Party. United States: Home Box Office (HBO).

3. David Zellerford, & Raymond De Felitta. April 25, 2012. Booker's Place: A Mississippi Story. United States: Eyepatch Productions.

4. http://www.urbandictionary.com/define.php?term=Woman+Child&defid=6 013855

5. https://www.wordnik.com/words/arrested%20development

Chapter 2

1. https://www.vocabulary.com/dictionary/survival

2. http://www.wordcentral.com/cgi-bin/student?va=survival

Chapter 3

3. http://dictionary.reference.com/browse/BASIC

4. Stacy Peralta. January 20, 2009. Crips and Bloods: Made in American. United States.

Chapter 4

1. Woodson, C.G. The Mis-Education of A Negro. (2006). ISBN# 156411041-9.

2. http://oxforddictionaries.com/definition/english/curse

3. http://www.urbandictionary.com/define.php?term=rebel

Chapter 6

1.
http://www.brainyquote.com/quotes/quotes/m/malcolmx386475.html   2.

http://www.merriam-webster.com/dictionary/ignorance

Chapter 7

1. Esposito, B. & Wood, J. (1982). *1935 Black Reconstruction in America* (p.149). New York: Hartcourt, Brace and Company.

2.http://en.wikipedia.org/wiki/Thirteenth_Amendment_to_the_United_S tates_Constitution

3. http://beck.library.emory.edu/southernchanges/article.php?id=sc223_ 020

4. http://eh.net/encyclopedia/slavery-in-the-united-states/

5. http://en.wikipedia.org/wiki/Convict_lease

6. Blackmon, Douglas A. *Slavery by Another Name: The Re-Enslavement of Black*

    Americans from the Civil War to World War II, (2008) ISBN 978-0-38550625-0, p. 4

7. http://en.wikipedia.org/wiki/Convict_lease

8.
    http://www.historyisaweapon.com/defcon1/gilmoreprisonslavery.html

9.
    http://www.historyisaweapon.com/defcon1/gilmoreprisonslavery.html

10. http://en.wikipedia.org/wiki/Black_Codes_(United_States)

11. http://en.wikipedia.org/wiki/Vagrancy_(people)

Chapter 8

1. Darin Scott, & Hughes Brothers. May 26, 1993. Menace II Society. USA: New Line

    Cinema.

Chapter 9

1. http://dictionary.reference.com/browse/system?s=t

Chapter 10

1. http://en.wikipedia.org/wiki/Education

2. http://www.forbes.com/sites/stevecohen/2010/12/25/a5childrensbook -vs-a- 47000-jail-cell-choose-one/

Chapter 11

1. United States Census Bureau. The National Data Book 131st Edition. Statistical Abstract of the United States: 2012.

Chapter 12

1. http://www.racismreview.com/blog/2015/05/12/blackssportsintegratio n-exploitation *Chapter 13*

1. http://www.brainyquote.com/quotes/quotes/d/davidcamer412890.html

2. http://oxforddictionaries.com/definition/english/welfare

3. http://www.thefreedictionary.com/welfare

4. http://oxforddictionaries.com/definition/english/assistance

5. Steven Nicolaides, & John Singleton. July 12, 1991. Boyz in The Hood. United States:

   Columbia Pictures.

6. http://oxforddictionaries.com/definition/english/detriment

7. Urban Dictionary, http://www.urbandictionary.com/projects (August 2013)

Chapter 14

1. Anne Moore & Michael Moore. October 2, 2009. Capitalism: A Love Story. Overture

    Films (US) & Paramount Vantage (international)

2. Jeffrey Silver, Bobby Newmyer, & Antoine Fuqua. October 5, 2001. Training Day. United States: Warner Bros. Pictures.

3. http://www.duhaime.org/LegalDictionary/B/BlackCode.aspx

4. http://www.drugpolicy.org/drug-facts/cocaine-and-crack-facts *Chapter 15*

1. http://en.wikipedia.org/wiki/Private_prison

2. http://en.wikipedia.org/wiki/Recidivism

3. http://www.thefreedictionary.com/rehabilitation

4. http://www.correctionsproject.com/corrections/pris_priv.htm

5. http://www.democracynow.org/2011/2/22/judge_convicted_in_pennsylvania_ kids_for

6. http://govtslaves.info/govt-guarantees-90-occupancyrateinprivateprisons/

7. http://rollingout.com/political-scandals/whatprivateprisonssuingstates-for- millions-if-they-dont-stay-full/

8. Anne Moore & Michael Moore. October 2, 2009. Capitalism: A Love Story. Overture

Films (US) & Paramount Vantage (international)

9. http://en.wikepedia.com/sweatshop

Chapter 16

1. http://www.great-quotes.com/quote/13182

Chapter 17

1. Peter Gatien, Jon Kilik, Jane Rosenthal, & Robert De Niro. September 29, 1993. A Brox

    Tales. US: Savoy Pictures

2. http://en.wikipedia.org/wiki/Glass_ceiling

3. Sofia Sondervan, Andrew Lack, Beyoncé Knowles, & Darnell Martin. December 5, 2008.

    Cadillac Records. United States: TriStar Pictures.

4. http://www.merriam-webster.com/dictionary/affirmative%20action

5. http://dictionary.reference.com/browse/insubordinate?s=t

Chapter 18

1. http://en.wikipedia.org/wiki/Unity_(disambiguation)

2. http://dictionary.reference.com/browse/power

Chapter 19

1. Walter Coblenz, Tracy Kramer, & Brett Ratner. August 22, 1997. Money Talks. United States:

New Line Cinema.

2. http://en.wikipedia.org/wiki/Greenwood,_Tulsa,_Oklahoma#.22The_Bl ack _Wall_

Street.22

3. http://www.youtube.com/watch?v=E70lf8jGr-A

4. Spike Lee, & Spike Lee. February 12, 1988. School Daze. United States: 40 Acres and a Mule Filmworks & Columbia Pictures

Chapter 20

1. http://jonathanturley.org/2012/05/20/propaganda-101whatyouneedto-know- and-why-or/

Made in the USA
Columbia, SC
13 May 2018